NEW DIRECTIONS FOR PHILANTHROPIC FUNDRAISING

Cathlene Williams
Association of Fundraising Professionals

Lilya Wagner
The Center on Philanthropy at Indiana University
COEDITORS-IN-CHIEF

EXPLORING MEASUREMENT AND EVALUATION EFFORTS IN FUNDRAISING

Mark A. Hager
Center on Nonprofits and Philanthropy, The Urban Institute

EDITOR

T0340138

NUMBER 41, FALL 2003

EXPLORING MEASUREMENT AND EVALUATION EFFORTS IN FUNDRAISING
Mark A. Hager (ed.)
New Directions for Philanthropic Fundraising, No. 41, Fall 2003
Cathlene Williams, Lilya Wagner, Coeditors-in-Chief

NEW DIRECTIONS FOR PHILANTHROPIC FUNDRAISING is indexed in Higher Education Abstracts and Philanthropic Index.

Microfilm copies of issues and articles are available in 16 mm and 35 mm, as well as microfiche in 105 mm, through University Microfilms Inc., 300 North Zeeb Road, Ann Arbor, Michigan 48106-1346.

ISSN 1072-172X (print)   ISSN 1542-7846 (online)

NEW DIRECTIONS FOR PHILANTHROPIC FUNDRAISING is part of the Jossey-Bass Nonprofit and Public Management Series and is published quarterly by Wiley Subscription Services, Inc., A Wiley company, at Jossey-Bass, 989 Market Street, San Francisco, California 94103-1741.

SUBSCRIPTIONS cost $109.00 for individuals and $215.00 for institutions, agencies, and libraries. Prices subject to change. Refer to the order form at the back of this issue.

EDITORIAL CORRESPONDENCE should be sent to Lilya Wagner, The Center on Philanthropy at Indiana University, 550 West North Street, Suite 301, Indianapolis, IN 46202-3162, or to Cathlene Williams, Association of Fundraising Professionals, 1101 King Street, Suite 700, Alexandria, VA 22314.

www.josseybass.com

Contents

Editor's Notes

NONPROFIT ORGANIZATIONS gain support by projecting an image of competency and legitimacy to their various constituencies. If a nonprofit projects nothing, it will wither. If it projects an image that conveys that it is other than an essential or outstanding contributor to those it serves, then it will garner only limited support. If it fails to project an image of worthiness and accountability, then supporters may shift their goodwill and other resources to a nonprofit's competitors. Consequently, many nonprofit organizations invest in high-dollar marketing efforts and hire charismatic executive directors to project an image that will attract contributions from their community. However, despite these fine efforts, the marketing and executive staffs of America's charities do not always control the public face of the organization. Often, the public faces of individual charities are built primarily by their accountants.

Accountants, you say? Accountants (and other financial management staffers) are responsible for maintaining systems for tracking and reporting costs and revenues in organizations. Information from this system is the basis for financial reports that get into the hands of donors, institutional funders, the Internal Revenue Service (IRS), the media, and nonprofit watchdog organizations. The public, it seems, has stumbled on a "quick and dirty" way to compare and evaluate the donation-worthiness of charities. For good or ill, these assessments are made from the bottom-line financial numbers reported by an unseen army of professional accountants and amateur treasurers. Donors want to give to organizations that they believe will use their money in a productive, project-oriented way. Although potential donors may never see the billboard or the CEO that an organization works so hard to get into the public eye,

NEW DIRECTIONS FOR PHILANTHROPIC FUNDRAISING, NO. 41, FALL 2003 © WILEY PERIODICALS, INC.

they do often see the organization's IRS Form 990 at the Web site of Philanthropic Research, Inc. (http://www.GuideStar.org), or they might see an organization ranked by financial efficiency in an annual issue of *Money* magazine or *US News & World Report*. The fates of these organizations are in the hands of those who track and report organizations' financial positions. In these cases, the impression of donation-worthiness is based primarily on financial efficacy rather than on effectiveness in program delivery.

One financial measure that the public has been trained to care about is fundraising efficiency, or the ratio of the amount of money spent on fundraising to the amount of money raised in contributions. When people hear stories that $35 of their $50 contribution goes back into next year's solicitations, that $10 of their contribution is used to pay for rent and electricity, and that only $5 goes to the cause that drove them to open their checkbooks, they get frustrated. However, the widespread availability of the information necessary to do these kinds of calculations has driven people to make giving decisions based exclusively on the measurement and evaluation of fundraising revenues and costs. To some donors, the cause matters less than the ability of an organization to demonstrate that it is a good steward of the money that the public entrusts to it. In turn, organizations begin to control their public *financial* face so that it projects the kind of image that attracts donors and grant makers while keeping watchdogs, regulators, and bad press at bay.

The chapters in this issue were solicited to address a variety of issues regarding the measurement and evaluation of fundraising costs and activities. In Chapter One, Jordan E. Silvergleid investigates the question of how much the public pays attention to the ratings of watchdog groups, evaluations that are based largely on organizational self-reports of program, fundraising, and administrative costs. This chapter is important because it points to a notable development in the evaluation of fundraising, namely the use of financial reports and other assessments to rate the worthiness of charities. Although Silvergleid does not report a relationship between watchdog ratings and contributions in his national sample, he raises important questions that follow in a line of research about the connections between external referents of organizational success and the supports that organizations receive.

One of the benefits of increased data collection among charities and their fundraising activities is greater potential for understanding the scope and dimensions of these activities. One kind of fundraising, workplace solicitation of federal employees in the Combined Federal Campaign, has escaped attention of nonprofit scholarship. Chapter Two, by Woods Bowman, is the first step in efforts to fill this gap. Bowman discusses recent giving patterns for both the national Combined Federal Campaign and the giving of federal employees in the Chicago area.

In Chapter Three, I report summary results from a national study of nonprofit fundraising and administrative costs. The impetus for this study, conducted by the Urban Institute in Washington, D.C., and the Center on Philanthropy at Indiana University, was the desire to benchmark how nonprofit organizations spend their money. However, as the study evolved, we became increasingly aware that the shortcomings of cost accounting result in poor financial information in many charities in the United States. Consequently, the project has been as much about the vagaries of financial reporting as it has been about actual amounts spent on particular administrative line items or different modes of fundraising. In this chapter, I discuss the current state of accounting for fundraising expenses in documents such as annual financial statements, the IRS Form 990, and grant reports—documents that funders use to divine whether organizations are worthy recipients of their charitable contributions.

Next, Terrence R. Colvin provides in Chapter Four his vision for using the price of outcomes to encourage funders to support particular social service delivery programs. He believes that the combination of specific prices for returns on investment and guarantees of success on these results will create a fundraising pitch that will increase venture philanthropy. At the center of his approach is the systematic measurement and evaluation of the efforts and outcomes of service providers.

Although most of the chapters in this volume are optimistic about current measurement efforts in learning about fundraising and donor behavior, Bill Levis is critical of the use of simple ratios to gauge fundraising efficiency and to ferret out abusive charities and professional fundraising firms. In Chapter Five, Levis describes the development of a fictional and wildly successful professional fundraising firm that puts its profit motive far ahead of its desire to further the charitable missions of its clients. He contends that "ill-intentioned fundraising abusers" of this sort blight the sector but that current regulatory mechanisms are not equipped to detect and deter them. He suggests that the answer lies not in measurement and evaluation but in the regulation of donor-list ownership.

Finally, a trio of nonprofit accounting professors, Elizabeth Keating, Linda Parsons, and Andrea Roberts, continues with the topic of professional fundraising firms. Whereas Levis's satire describes a firm that returns little money to its nonprofit clients, Keating, Parsons, and Roberts (Chapter Six) describe data from New York that show that most professional solicitation firms keep most of the contributions in most campaigns. They present a series of questions about telemarketing campaigns and then use their New York data to shed light on the answers. The result is a clear indication of why the low yields to charities continue to be a hot issue in nonprofitdom.

Taken together, the chapters in this volume reflect three major themes in the evaluation and measurement of fundraising today. First, research on fundraising has the definite benefit of teaching students of the field what the field looks like. The chapters by Bowman and by Keating, Parsons, and Roberts use descriptive data to give us an informed picture of several major dimensions of fundraising.

The second theme regards the quality of the information we have when we seek to measure and evaluate charities and their fundraising activities. If we want to draw conclusions about fundraising activities, or if we want to rank charities based on how well they do something, then we need to feel good about the information we are using to draw our conclusions. I indicate that financial ratios are based on numbers generated from questionable accounting practices, whereas Colvin advocates the calculation of prices from difficult social-accounting computations. Both efficiency ratios and prices rely on numbers that most nonprofits simply are not prepared to supply with reliability.

The third theme concerns the kinds of decisions people make from evaluations of fundraising. Silvergleid begins with the popular hypothesis that donors care about how nonprofit organizations spend their money and that they pay attention to the rankings and ratings published by nonprofit watchdog organizations. Levis criticizes the common use of ratios to assess whether charities and their professional fundraisers are donation-worthy or not. Both point to the pervasive use of financial measures to assess what organizations do and how well they do it. Due to the lack of information that allows us to assess the quality of programs and how effective nonprofits are in carrying out their charitable goals, stakeholders fall back on financial information as a proxy. The result is that the bottom line and financial efficiency have become the measures by which we assess charities in the United States. In many ways, the image of the sector and its individual nonprofits is in the hands of their bookkeepers.

Mark A. Hager
Editor

MARK A. HAGER *is a research associate in the Center on Nonprofits and Philanthropy at the Urban Institute, a social policy research organization in Washington, D.C.*

This chapter examines the effects that watchdog agency evaluations of nonprofit organizations have on private donations.

1

Effects of watchdog organizations on the social capital market

Jordan E. Silvergleid

ONE OF THE LONG-TERM residual effects of the "dot-com" boom may be found in the "dot-org" world. In the late 1990s, successful entrepreneurs and investors, flush with initial public offerings and stock-option winnings, began to practice "venture philanthropy" and invest in "social entrepreneurs," hoping to replicate their business success in the social sector. Their results-oriented rhetoric, combined with several high-profile nonprofit financial scandals, contributed to calls for nonprofit accountability and a more efficient "social capital market," in which charitable donations would flow to the most effective organizations, whether large or small (Meehan, 2002). Over the next several years, scholars and practitioners focused on identifying and quantifying nonprofit measures of performance to spur its development (Roberts Enterprise Development Fund, 2000; Murray, 2001). Today, accountability and performance measurement are part of most discussions about the future of the nonprofit sector.

Note: The author wishes to thank Felix Oberholzer-Gee of Harvard Business School and Tom Pollak and Kendall Golladay of the National Center for Charitable Statistics, Urban Institute, for their invaluable contributions to this project.

But is such a social capital market feasible? Even if it were possible to develop accurate and comparable metrics, would many donors (besides a few vocal venture philanthropists) necessarily shift their funding to higher-performing organizations?

Foundations of giving

Of the $241 billion that was given to nonprofit organizations in 2000, 11 percent came from foundations, 4 percent came from corporate sources, 5 percent came from bequests, and more than 76 percent came from individuals (AAFRC Trust for Philanthropy, 2003). What factors drive the flow of this money to specific organizations, particularly the more than three-quarters donated by individuals? Such knowledge is clearly desirable to fundraisers, especially given the much-heralded intergenerational transfer of wealth that, according to one estimate, will raise giving by $100 billion to $150 billion a year by 2010 (Smith, 2002). Numerous research studies have explored the factors that lead individuals to donate, including religious philosophy, social responsibility, "fellow-feeling," the need to give back (or get back), enjoyment, and family influence. Schervish and Havens (1997) found that charitable giving increases in direct relation to the greater involvement one has in "communities of participation," the more frequently and personally one is asked to contribute, the greater the number and intensity of charitable modeling in one's youth, and the greater the amount of discretionary resources.

Yet, how important is nonprofit efficiency and performance to donor selection, factors that would ostensibly be the linchpin of a well-functioning social capital market? Although research on nonprofit performance has been hampered by inherent measurement difficulties, two primary lines of inquiry have been undertaken into the value placed on efficiency: public opinion surveys and empirical analysis of giving behavior. (In a third approach not discussed here, Parsons [2001] conducted a field experiment and found that prospective donors were more likely to make a contribution when efficiency measures were provided directly with request funds. In another simulation, Parsons found that an average donation was greater when information about service efforts and accomplishments was provided.) Public opinion surveys have shown strong donor interest in how organizations use their contributions. A 1988 Roper Organization survey found that the amount spent for programs was the second most important factor in the decision to contribute to a nonprofit, a factor that was rated as important or very important by 82 percent of respondents (Glaser, 1994). A later study from the Hudson Institute on the attitudes Americans have toward public charities found that nearly half of the respondents said that how much the recipient organizations spend on administration and fundraising influences their giving decisions (Stehle, 1998). Finally, according to a Better Business Bureau (BBB) Wise Giving Alliance Donor Expectations Survey (Princeton Survey Research Associates, 2001), respondents who say they are inclined to seek information about a charity before contributing are asked to describe in their own words what they most want to know. Close to half (48 percent) volunteer something related to charity finances, more than twice the number who specifically mentions any other issue. In addition, 79 percent of respondents in this study say it is very important to know the percentage of spending that goes toward charitable programs.

Given that survey results may reflect what individuals *prefer to think* are the factors that drive their donation decisions, empirical analysis of giving behavior may be more telling. Weisbrod and Dominguez (1986) developed a model relating donations to fundraising efficiency, fundraising efforts, and type of organization. Examining a sample of nonprofit organizations that file Internal Revenue Service (IRS) Form 990 for the four years 1973 through 1976, they found that fundraising expenditures exert two countervailing effects on donations: the direct effect (advertising and information) augments donations, but the indirect effect (by increasing the price of donating) reduces donations. The overall effect, however, is not significantly different from zero. Additional studies (Posnett and Sandler, 1989; Callen, 1994; Tinkelman, 1998; Okten and Weisbrod, 2000) support this conclusion with other data sets (from the United Kingdom, Canada, and New York State) and different time periods.

Frumkin and Kim (2001) asked a similar question: is financial efficiency rewarded by donors? They examined Form 990 data from 1985 through 1995 and found that reporting low ratios of administrative to total expense and positioning an organization as efficient do not lead to greater success in garnering contributions; instead, nonprofit organizations that spend more in marketing themselves to the public (that is, through higher fundraising costs) do better at raising contributed income. They conclude that "strategic positioning through the aggressive communication of mission is a more potent driver of contributions than maintaining efficient operations" (p. 16).

Although it may appear at first that Frumkin and Kim's findings contradict previous research, this is not entirely clear. Frumkin and Kim fail to consider how increasing fundraising costs may exert a lagged negative effect on contributions. Indeed, their measure of efficiency focuses on administrative costs as a percentage of total costs rather than administrative *and* fundraising costs, a combined percentage that donors appear to care about deeply. Another hypothesis that Frumkin and Kim (and other researchers) fail to explore is that although donors may care about efficiency, they may not care enough to overcome the search costs associated with procuring adequate financial information. After all, before GuideStar made Form 990 information available online (http://www.guidestar.org) in the late 1990s, donors would have to specifically request this information from potential donation recipients. Even in 2001, "many, if not most, Americans have trouble finding information they need to evaluate charities and make decisions about giving" (Princeton Survey Research Associates, 2001, p. 4). When they need information to make decisions about giving, only 49 percent of respondents say it is easy to find what they are looking for. And whereas people's main source of information to help make giving decisions is charities themselves, only 50 percent of those surveyed credits charities with making the appropriate information available.

Enter the watchdogs

In response to concerns about nonprofit accountability and the scarcity of information (among other factors), a handful of organizations has emerged to help donors navigate the charitable universe. As Table 1.1 illustrates, each organization scrutinizes charities according to selected criteria and either assigns them an overall grade or indicates that they have met its guidelines (in sum or in part). Although criteria vary, most organizations pay close attention to financial measures, such as percentage of funds dedicated to programs, fundraising, and administration and how much money the charity has in reserves (watchdogs dislike excessive stockpiling). Although no organization currently examines the effects of a charity's programs, several look to see if the charity has an evaluation program in place.

The oldest and most venerable groups to evaluate charities are the National Charities Information Bureau and the Council for Better Business Bureau, which merged in 2001 to become the BBB Wise Giving Alliance. Both the original organizations and the newly merged group take a binary approach (charities either pass or do not pass the list of standards) and oppose the idea that they are "rating" charities. In contrast, the American Institute of Philanthropy (AIP) has assigned letter grades to charities since 1993 and often reallocates charities' program expenses (such as "educational" mailings) as fundraising expenditures. Other organizations focus their efforts on certain states (Minnesota and Maryland) or subsectors (such as Ministry Watch, which rates some four hundred Christian organizations). In the past few years, financial publications such as *Worth*, *Forbes*, and *Smart Money* have begun to provide annual guides of charities to help their readers. Among the newest entrants is Charity Navigator, an ambitious watchdog that

Table 1.1. Watchdog agencies

Name	Evaluated Charities Since	Cycle Time	Groups Evaluated	Rating Metrics	Criteria	How Charities Are Selected
Council of Better Business Bureaus (CBBB)	Better Business Bureau (BBB) system founded in 1912; current charity guidelines established in 2001	Regularly updated	N.A.	Organizations either meet each standard or do not	Public accountability Use of funds Solicitations and materials Fundraising practices Governance	Charities evaluated based on number of individual requests; these standards apply to publicly soliciting organizations that are tax exempt under section 501 (C) (3) of the IRS Code and to other organizations conducting charitable solicitations
National Charities Information Bureau (NCIB)	1992; merged in 2001 with CBBB to form BBB Wise Giving Alliance	Regularly updated	N.A.	Organizations either meet each standard or do not	Governance Purpose Programs Information Financial support and related activities Use of funds Annual reporting Accountability Budget	NCIB believes the spirit of these standards is useful for all charities; however, for organizations less than three years old or with annual budgets of less than $100,000, greater flexibility in applying some of the standards may be appropriate
BBB Wise Giving Alliance	2001, result of merger between NCIB and CBBB	Regularly updated quarterly publication	N.A.	Indicates whether or not charity meets each of the standards	Governance standards Measuring effectiveness Finances Fundraising and informational materials Address privacy concerns of donors	In response to inquiries from the general public, businesses, and other potential donors, provides impartial reports on organizations that conduct national or international fundraising or program services; in addition to reports on individual organizations, the alliance publishes the *Better Business Bureau Wise Giving Guide*,

Organization	Year	Frequency	Number rated	Rating scale	Criteria	Description
American Institute of Philanthropy (AIP)	1993	Triannual	N.A.	Letter grade (A, B, C, D, F)	Percentage spent on programs: 60 percent and more is "reasonable" Cost to raise $100: $35 or less is "reasonable" Years of available assets: reserve of less than three years is "reasonable"	AIP strives "to cover many of the groups that AIP members are most interested in; it requires "that the organization's programs be of interest to donor nationally and that its annual budget be at least $500,000"; AIP does not report on churches, synagogues, mosques, political action committees, fraternal clubs, colleges, or local institutions, such as hospitals and museums; it does report on the separate human and social welfare organizations of religious groups
Charity Navigator	2001	Regularly updated	1,750 and growing	Four-star scale (with associated numerical rating)	Short-term spending practices Long-term sustainability	Evaluates the 1,750 largest charities that provide all types of programs in all parts of the country that are tax exempt and that seek donations from individual givers; to grow its database, Charity Navigator adds the largest organizations with the largest percentage of individual donations with special priority to underrepresented regions or sectors (health, international); to be evaluated, charities must also provide thirty-six consecutive months of Form 990 filings

a quarterly magazine listing national charitable organizations generating the greatest number of inquiries through its office

(continued)

Table 1.1. *(continued)*

Name	Evaluated Charities Since	Cycle Time	Groups Evaluated	Rating Metrics	Criteria	How Charities Are Selected
Ministry Watch	2000	N.A.	400	Assigns financial efficiency rating (five-star rating); assigns transparency grade (A–F); provides in-depth analyst comments on each ministry and subsector	Financial efficiency rating is assessed in terms of Fund acquisition Resource allocation Asset utilization Transparency grade is assessed in terms of Responsiveness Disclosure	400 largest Christian ministries in the United States
Maryland Association of Nonprofits' Standards for Excellence	1999	Self-selection	30	Binary: meets all criteria (and receives seal of excellence) or does not	Mission and program Governing body Conflict of interest Human resources Financial and legal Openness Fundraising Public affairs and public policy	Offers a voluntary, peer-review, certification program for nonprofit organizations interested in demonstrating that they carry out the Standards for Excellence; organizations that prove compliance become certified; to participate, organizations must submit a written application, provide documentation, and pay an application fee; panel of trained peer reviewers assesses the applicant's practices and determines if the standards have been met; certified organizations are given permission to use the Seal of Excellence, a symbol the public and donors alike can trust

Charities Review Council of Minnesota	Active in Minnesota since 1946; it standards revised in 1998 after two years of discussion and input from funders nonprofits, accountants, and individual donors	Regularly updated (a review is considered current for three years)	About 600	Organizations either meet all council standards or do not meet one or more standards	Public disclosure Governance Financial activity Fundraising	Initiates reviews with those charities about which the greatest number of inquiries are received; occasionally will also review a charity at its own request or at the request of a foundation
SmartMoney Magazine	2000	Annual	100	Total score and ranking within subsector (conservation, culture, and the like)	Program ratio: percentage of budget that goes toward program activities (65 percent weight in scoring) Fundraising ratio: how much it takes to raise $1 (25 percent weight in scoring) Savings ratio: percentage of incoming revenues that charity saves (10 percent weight in scoring)	100 largest charities in revenue

(continued)

Table 1.1. (continued)

Name	Evaluated Charities Since	Cycle Time	Groups Evaluated	Rating Metrics	Criteria	How Charities Are Selected
Forbes Magazine	2000	Annual	200	Calculates ratios and identifies direction of trend from previous year	Program ratio: percentage of budget that goes toward program activities Donor dependency: share of nonprofit's surplus coming from contributions, as opposed to sale of goods or investment performance Fundraising efficiency: percentage of funds raised from gifts that remains after subtracting fund-raising expenses	200 largest charities in revenue
Worth Magazine	2000	Annual	100	Inclusion on list of "best charities" or not	Each year, interviews "philanthropy experts" to develop a preliminary list of 200 national and international organizations that are nonpolitical To be included on final list, each organization must have a three-year track record and spend 65 percent on programs	

Note: N.A. refers to not available; IRS refers to Internal Revenue Service.

seeks to provide comprehensive ratings (on a four-star and numerical scale) for 1,750 nonprofit organizations free of charge. Finally, for donors who pay a $1,000 fee, the Philanthropy Group, a Chicago company started in 2002, conducts site visits and prepares in-depth reports. GuideStar is also considering expanding its fee-based service to provide more in-depth comparisons of charities based on their missions, geography, size, and history.

Although many have applauded the sunlight that these organizations bring to the nonprofit sector, others have been both skeptical and critical. Specifically, critics contend that the standard metrics (such as financial ratios) do not tell the "whole story" and cannot be compared across different types of organizations. Indeed, one recent study found that nonprofit overhead costs and fundraising-efficiency ratios differ significantly with organizational size and subsector (Hager, Pollak, and Rooney, 2002). To address this claim, watchdogs hedge their evaluations with cautionary prose and encourage donors to perform more extensive due diligence. Others develop a charity's overall ranking by comparing its ratios with those of subsector peers. In a recent chapter, Hopkins (2002) accused watchdog agencies of setting arbitrary and flawed standards (some of which disregard existing laws), of lacking the proper training and experience to effectively evaluate charities, and of falsely portraying themselves as neutral bodies applying voluntary standards (which are not, Hopkins contends, voluntary at all). All of these actions, Hopkins writes, "can cause great damage to charities that depend on public goodwill and financial support" (p. 446).

To date, however, little empirical research has specifically examined the effect that rankings and ratings have on charitable giving. To the extent that watchdogs reduce search costs for donors interested in efficiency, ratings might be expected to have an effect on contributions, in which case concerns about the appropriateness of their metrics might be warranted. At the same time, rankings may have no effect, leading to the conclusion that either they do not have enough visibility, that donors are "correctly" using such rankings only as a starting point, or that donors actually care less about efficiency than they claim in surveys.

I decided to test this question using ratings data from a national watchdog agency and from a more narrowly focused body, as well as information on contributions to the rated organizations (nationally focused and regionally focused charities, respectively). I was curious to see if there might be any difference between the two donor groups and hypothesized that donors giving to locally based and locally focused charities might be more motivated to obtain and consider the ratings assigned by a local watchdog.

Data and methods

It is surprisingly (and ironically) difficult to procure historical evaluation data from nationally focused watchdog agencies, which cite concerns over confidentiality, cumbersome filing, or lack of interest in providing such data. Nevertheless, I was able to obtain and examine AIP's quarterly ratings for the years 1997 through 2000, which were published and distributed as part of its *Charity Rating Guide*. (For information on the guide, see www.charitywatch.org.) Across this time period, AIP rated between 307 and 368 public charities on a scale of A through F. In each report, AIP lists all organizations with new or still current grades broken down into thirty-seven subsectors such as AIDS or international development. For each organization, AIP identifies whether the evaluation is new, whether the organization was willing to provide data, the percentage spent on program services, the cost to raise $100, and a final letter grade. Each quarter, AIP evaluated or reevaluated about 20 percent of the organizations listed in each guide; moreover, nearly every nonprofit in the data set was reevaluated at least once. According to organizational literature, AIP periodically reevaluates nonprofits based on membership interest or the passage of time.

Locally focused charity ratings for the same period (1997 through 2000) were easier to obtain from the Minnesota Charities Review Council (CRC). Twice a year, the CRC publishes a list of organizations (both Minnesota-based and national groups) and the extent to which each organization meets its list of standards, ranging from public disclosure to governance to financial activity. Of the approximately four hundred organizations evaluated across this time period, I identified 159 as being locally focused. This group includes state-based affiliates of national organizations, such as the Alliance for the Mentally Ill of Minnesota, as well as organizations with state-based headquarters and focus, such as Twin Cities Neighborhood Housing Services. Similar to AIP, CRC conducts reevaluations periodically, although it does not indicate which organizations have received a new evaluation.

For 95 percent of nationally focused organizations and 80 percent of Minnesota-based organizations, I obtained information provided to the IRS for one or more of the years 1997 through 2000 from the National Center for Charitable Statistics at the Urban Institute. Missing data appeared to be random, thus minimizing the possibility of selection bias. Nine organizations exhibiting questionable data were excluded, such as those reporting no private contributions in one year but large contributions in a subsequent year.

The model

Using two regression models, I sought to determine the effect that watchdog agency ratings have on private donations. The first model analyzes the extent to which a rating in the current period (1998, for example) drives contributions in the next period (1999) and thus assumes that ratings have a lagged effect on donations. The second model seeks to determine whether a reevaluation (which, in AIP's case, might result in a lower, higher, or the same grade) has a significant effect on future donations. In other words, I tested whether charities that receive an A grade can expect higher donations than organizations that receive a C and also whether a charity that earns better grades over time can expect to see a corresponding increase in private donations. To facilitate this analysis, both models control for certain variables: net assets (because large organizations could naturally expect to receive more contributions than small organizations), year (because donors may have been more or less generous depending on the prevailing economic environment), and subsector (because social problems often have different levels of support, regardless of the performance of the charity). I also tested each model while controlling for much more specific organizational characteristics to neutralize the fundraising effect of a charismatic or dull executive director or a successful public relations campaign.[1]

Results

Effect of AIP (national level) ratings on private donation levels

Results from the first regression model demonstrate that AIP grades do not have a positive effect on private donations in the subsequent period. In fact, when controlling for year, subsector, and net assets, higher AIP grades actually drive lower private contributions, although by an extremely small amount.

Should these results be interpreted, therefore, that organizations should seek to earn lower grades? In fact, no. Variations of the regression model indicate that net assets, certain subsectors, and organizational-specific factors are the significant predictors of private donations in this model and that AIP grade appears to be significant only under certain conditions. Statistical significance in regressions measures the ability of the variable to explain the residual effect after taking into account all the other variables in the equation. If, as appears to be the case, those other variables (such as net assets) do a good job of explanation, then there is not as much unexplained variation left in the residual data as there was in the original data. Consequently, AIP grades do not have to be as strongly associated with private donations to rise to a level of statistical significance.

Results from the second model, which tests whether a reevaluation (resulting in a lower, higher, or similar grade) affects private donations in the subsequent period, indicate that there is no significant link. In fact, among the variables tested, only net assets reasonably predicted the change in donations, perhaps supporting the claim that "it takes money to make money." Nevertheless, and unfortunately for fundraisers, this second model is not useful for explaining changes in private donations. (Statistically, this model has an adjusted multivariate coefficient of determination of .02; 1.00 would indicate that the model has 100 percent explanatory power.) Overall, then, as can be seen in Table 1.2, AIP grades do not have a statistically significant effect on private donations.

Effect of CRC (local) evaluations on private donation levels

A similar analysis was performed for Minnesota-based organizations using data from CRC. As can be seen in Table 1.3, results from the regression model indicate that grade (defined as meeting or not meeting all of CRC's standards) does have a significant positive effect on donations when asset size, year, and subsector are controlled. Organizations that met standards were more likely to earn higher donations in subsequent periods than those that did not meet standards. As with nationally focused charities, net assets are also a significant predictor of private contributions. In contrast, subsector is not a significant predictor, although this can perhaps be explained by the use of eleven subsector codes as opposed to AIP's thirty-seven industry segments.

Does this mean, then, that donors are more apt to scrutinize—and base their giving on—evaluations of local charities? To such a question, we can answer only tentatively in the affirmative, if at all.

Table 1.2. What drives private contributions to nationally focused charities?

Variable tested	Statistically significant predictor?	If yes, positive or negative effect?
Grade by AIP	No[a]	
Net assets	Yes	Positive
Year	No	
Subsector	Only certain subsectors	Depends
Charity-specific characteristics	Yes	Depends

[a]In certain variations of the regression model, AIP grade demonstrates a statistically significant impact on donations (both positive and negative). Overall, though, the effect is not significantly different from zero.

Table 1.3. What drives private contributions to regionally focused charities?

Variable tested	Statistically significant predictor?	If yes, positive or negative effect?
Evaluation by CRC	Yes	Positive
Net assets	Yes	Positive
Year	No	
Subsector	No	
Charity-specific characteristics	Yes	Depends

Of the 125 organizations in the data set, 86 percent received perfect evaluations across all four years, and presumably their performance had been consistent in previous years as well. Therefore it becomes more difficult to draw a strong causal link between evaluations and donations because these high-performing (by CRC standards) charities might have enjoyed strong reputations (and relationships with donors) for many years. Put simply, the CRC evaluation might be a less critical component to the giving process for these organizations. Moreover, only six organizations experienced changing evaluations (both positive and negative), which is too small a sample to draw conclusions about whether changing evaluations affected donations in subsequent periods. Thus, although the extant data suggest that contributions to locally based and focused nonprofits are driven in a significant manner by ratings assigned by a locally based and focused watchdog agency, it is perhaps wise to claim directional accuracy rather than a firm conclusion.

Discussion and conclusions

What can we make of these findings that, one, grades assigned by a national watchdog agency (AIP) to national charities are not a significant predictor of private donations, and that, two, evaluations of Minnesota-based and -focused charities by a state-based watchdog agency (CRC) appear to be a significant predictor of private dona-tions? The conservative response to both findings would be "not much." Clearly, a larger data set would provide more robust con-clusions, particularly in the case of locally focused organizations.

Regarding the first finding, it is important to state clearly that the results of this analysis indicate that AIP grades assigned to non-profits did not significantly drive giving patterns across the studied time period. However, the analysis does not explain why this is the case. It could be that some donors are highly responsive to ratings but that not enough are aware of them to make a significant dif-ference. It might also be that donors are aware and interested in such grades but that their giving patterns are relatively inelastic when it comes to minor changes in grades (such as from an A to an A minus). Thus, only if a nonprofit experienced a drastic change in grade would we see a corollary change in private contributions. Another possibility is that (following the stated intentions of a number of nonprofit-watchdog groups) donors use grades as a launching pad and correctly realize both that financial ratios do not necessarily correlate with effectiveness and that programmatic expenses and fundraising costs may vary dramatically across orga-nizations based on social cause and organizational age or size. Thus, although grades might be noted, they are simply one of a number of factors that influence the giving process, if they influ-ence it at all. Finally, it is possible that whereas donors are aware of these ratings, they do not take them into account, perhaps because they disagree with the metrics or prioritize other factors, such as mission or personal relationships.

Regarding the second finding, although it is a theoretically attractive proposition to state that local donors pay more attention to local ratings of local charities, the condition of the data casts some doubt on this tidy conclusion. Moreover, as Angela Bies, for-mer executive director of CRC, found in a previous survey of Min-nesota organizations (2001), less than half of respondents shared review data with funders, and a number indicated that "too few donors know about or use the council's services" (p. 65). What this second finding may suggest, however, is that CRC's nearly sixty years of operations have contributed to a high degree of standards compliance for the state's major charities.

This conclusion begs the question of whether nonprofit organizations themselves respond to grades and evaluations. Here it is important to distinguish between AIP's evaluation, which focuses on financial measures, and CRC's, which involves a more comprehensive review process. According to the Bies survey of Minnesota-based organizations, respondents (nearly all of whom met all standards) reported making changes in several areas as a result of the review process: governance (36 percent), communications (35 percent), management (28 percent), fundraising (22 percent), financial management (17 percent), and strategic planning (13 percent) (Bies, 2001). And yet, among the eighteen organizations that did not meet CRC's standards in this data set, thirteen did not subsequently improve their evaluations in later reviews. Moreover, a review of AIP reevaluations of organizations earning less than an A across the sample period revealed that 75 percent were the "same" or "decrease[d]." Because the components of these grades are more or less endogenous, these statistics seem to imply that organizations are not motivated to improve their standing with watchdogs.

Thus, for the moment, it appears that any concerns about the power of watchdog agencies to shape contribution patterns are unwarranted. The findings also suggest that the much-vaunted "efficient social capital market" appears to be at least several years off. Also of note is that the period under study here (1997 through 2000) was an economic heyday when efficiency of nonprofit organizations may have been less of an issue for donors. In these leaner economic times, philanthropists may become more vigilant about their donations and more responsive to the increasing number of watchdog agencies and "top nonprofit" lists. Additional individual incentives to give to "efficient" groups may emerge. Watchdog agencies may successfully incorporate effectiveness measures into their evaluations. Regardless of one's perspective on these possible changes, ensuring that watchdog agencies appeal to donor interests while educating them on important metrics certainly seems important. At the same time, they must recognize differences among nonprofits while striving for comparability.

Note

1. The two models used to determine the effect on private donations can be described as follows:

$$
\begin{aligned}
\ln\text{Don}(t) = {} & C(0) + B(1)\text{grade}(t - 1) \\
& + B(2)\text{organizational characteristics}(t - 1) \\
& + B(3)\text{year}(t) + u(i) \text{ and} \\
\text{Change Don}(t) = {} & C(0) + B(1)\text{change grade}(t - 1) \\
& + B(2)\text{organizational characteristics}(t - 1) \\
& + B(3)\text{year}(t) + u(i)
\end{aligned}
$$

where *lnDon* is the natural logarithm of the dollar amount of contributions (calculated as total contributions minus government contributions); *grade* is the numerical grade or rating in the previous period; *Change Don* is the change in private contributions; *Change grade* is the change in grade in the previous period; *organizational characteristics* included (1) subsector, (2) natural logarithm of net assets, (3) sector and ln (net assets), or (4) organization; *year* is the year of donations; and $u(i)$ is distributed independently. To facilitate the analysis, AIP evaluations were quantified (A+ = 13, A = 12 . . . F = 0), as were the evaluations given by CRC ("meets all standards" = 1, and "does not meet all standards" = 0).

References

AAFRC Trust for Philanthropy. *Giving USA 2003: The Annual Report on Philanthropy for the Year 2002*. Indianapolis, IN: AAFCR, 2003.

Bies, A. L. "Accountability, Organizational Capacity, and Continuous Improvement: Findings From Minnesota's Nonprofit Sector." In P. Barber (ed.), Accountability: A Challenge for Charities and Fundraisers. *New Directions for Philanthropic Fundraising*, no. 31. San Francisco: Jossey-Bass, 2001, pp. 51–80.

Callen, J. "Money Donations, Volunteering, and Organizational Efficiency." *Journal of Productivity Analysis*, 1994, *5*, 215–228.

Frumkin, P., and Kim, M. "Strategic Positioning and the Financing of Nonprofit Organizations: Is Efficiency Rewarded in the Contributions Marketplace?" *Public Administration Review*, 2001, *61*(3), 266–275.

Glaser, J. S. *The United Way Scandal: An Insider's Account of What Went Wrong and Why*. New York: Wiley, 1994.

Greenlee, J. S., and Brown, K. L. "The Impact of Accounting Information on Contributions to Charitable Organizations." *Research in Accounting Regulation*, 1999, *13*, 111–125.

Hager, M., Pollak, T., and Rooney, P. "Variations in Overhead and Fundraising Efficiency Measures: The Influence of Size, Age, and Subsector."

Working Paper. Center on Nonprofits and Philanthropy at the Urban Institute and Center on Philanthropy at Indiana University, 2002. [http.www.coststudy.org].

Hopkins, B. R. "Standards Enforcement by Watchdog Agencies. In *The Law of Fundraising*. New York: Wiley, 2002.

Meehan, W. F. "Reforming the Social Capital Market." Unpublished manuscript, San Francisco: McKinsey and Co., 2002.

Murray, V. "The State of Evaluation Tools and Systems for Nonprofit Organizations." In P. Barber (ed.), *Accountability: A Challenge for Charities and Fundraisers*. New Directions for Philanthropic Fundraising, no. 31, San Francisco: Jossey-Bass, 2001, pp. 39–49.

Okten, C., and Weisbrod, B. A. "Determinants of Donations in Private Nonprofit Markets." *Journal of Public Economics*, 2000, *75*, 255–272.

Parsons, L. M. "The Impact of Financial Information and Voluntary Disclosures on Contributions to Not-for-Profit Organizations: A Field-Based Experiment." Unpublished doctoral dissertation, Bauer College of Business at the University of Houston, 2001.

Posnett, J., and Sandler, T. "Demand for Charity Donations in Private Non-Profit Markets. The Case of the U.K." *Journal of Public Economics*, 1989, *40*, 187–200.

Princeton Survey Research Associates. *Final Report: BBB Wise Giving Alliance Donor Expectations Survey: Final Report*. Princeton, N.J.: Princeton Survey Research Associates, 2001.

Roberts Enterprise Development Fund. "Social Return on Investment Collection." 2000. [http://www.redf.org/pub_sroi.htm].

Schervish, P. G., and Havens, J. J. "Social Participation and Charitable Giving: A Multivariate Analysis." *Voluntas: International Journal of Voluntary and Nonprofit Organizations*, 1997, *8*(3), 235–260.

Smith, E. "The Coming Flood: Philanthropy in This Decade." *Global Business Network*. 2000. [http://www.gbn.org].

Stehle, V. "Study: Americans Confident in Charities' Integrity." *Chronicle of Philanthropy*, Sept. 10, 1998, *10*(22), pp. 5–12.

Tinkelman, D. "Differences in Sensitivity of Financial Statement Users to Joint Cost Allocations: The Case of Nonprofit Organizations." *Journal of Accounting, Auditing, and Finance*, Fall 1998, pp. 377–393.

Tinkelman, D. "Factors Affecting the Relation Between Donations to Not-for-Profit Organizations and an Efficiency Ratio." *Research in Government and Nonprofit Accounting*, 1999, *10*, 135–161.

Weisbrod, B. A., and Dominguez, N. D. "Demand for Collective Goods in Private Nonprofit Markets: Can Fundraising Expenditures Help Overcome Free-Rider Behavior?" *Journal of Public Economics*, 1986, *30*, 83–96.

JORDAN E. SILVERGLEID *is a director of strategic planning at The Advisory Board Company in Washington, D.C. He completed this work while an MBA student at The Wharton School of Business at the University of Pennsylvania.*

The Combined Federal Campaign gives federal workers an opportunity to contribute to local charities by payroll deduction. This article provides an overview of the size and scope of this program.

2

Workplace giving: A case study of the Combined Federal Campaign

Woods Bowman

"WHICH WOULD BE easier? Asking someone to give you $50? Or asking this person to give you $1 a week? Clearly the latter, and that is a key reason why workplace fundraising is being seen by more and more organizations today as a new source of private revenues" (National Committee for Responsive Philanthropy, 1997, p. 1). As the nation's largest employer, the federal government is a good place to begin a study of workplace giving. In this chapter, I look at the basic data on campaign costs, amounts given, types of charities supported, and the charities' administrative and fundraising costs. I offer such evidence as can be found to shed light on questions such as: Are large campaigns more efficient than small ones? Are large campaigns more successful? Are more successful campaigns more expensive? Do workplace campaigns disproportionately benefit local charities?

The Combined Federal Campaign (CFC) is the sole authorized annual workplace fundraising campaign within the federal government. The organization's helpful Web site, from which most of my background material on the CFC is drawn, can be found at

NEW DIRECTIONS FOR PHILANTHROPIC FUNDRAISING, NO. 41, FALL 2003 © WILEY PERIODICALS, INC.

http://www.opm.gov.cfc. Federal employees may designate a specific charitable organization to receive their contribution, and they may choose whether to make a lump-sum payment or give through payroll deduction. The 2002 campaign attracted over 1.3 million individual contributors.

A brief history

Before 1956, charitable giving in federal workplaces was unsystematic and, in places, chaotic. In that year, the President's Advisor on Personnel Management laid out general guidelines for when and how charitable campaigns should be conducted in the federal workplace. The first solicitation under these rules took place in 1958, with a select few charities participating. Initially there were three campaigns a year, organized by type of charity.

In 1964, the CFC concept was piloted in six cities under its current name. "The result was a substantial increase in contributions, ranging from 20 percent to 125 percent, and a highly favorable response within the federal community" (Combined Federal Campaign, n.d.). President Nixon made CFC the uniform fundraising method for the federal service.

Participating charities were added slowly, rising to just thirty-three in 1979. In deciding *Natural Resources Defense Council* v. *Campbell*, the U.S. District Court for the District of Columbia opened the doors to other charities. By 1984, practically any public charity was eligible. The following year, President Reagan promulgated an executive order that excluded advocacy, legal defense, and other organizations that were not health and welfare related. The following year, the U.S. Supreme Court upheld his action.

Public Law 100–202 (1988), effective with the 1992 campaign, created the CFC we know today. It expanded local eligibility by defining and enumerating criteria for organizations that provide services on a statewide basis and removed all general designation options not required by statute. Today, thousands of charities participate in the CFC. In Chicago alone, about eighteen hundred participate.

How it works

CFC is a conglomerate of 376 local campaigns. Each campaign is conducted in a federal administrative region under the aegis of a local federal coordinating committee (LFCC), which brings together top local officials, taking care to include military, civil service, and postal service leaders. In the twenty-eight cities where they operate, federal executive boards fill the role of the LFCC. LFCCs implement the law and regulations advanced by the federal Office of Personnel Management (OPM). OPM determines whether national and international charities are eligible to receive funds, and each of the 376 local LFCCs determines eligibility of charities in their local areas. The LFCCs select a vendor to handle the mechanics of the operation, known as a principal combined fund organization (PCFO). These organizations conduct the local campaigns, encouraging charitable donations, informing employees of their giving options, and getting the gifts into the right hands.

The PCFO gives each employee a donor's guide, which is a catalogue of charities eligible to receive funds through CFC. Each guide gives important information on every eligible local, national, and international organization, including organization name, telephone number, Web address, federal EIN (Employer Identification Number), a twenty-five-word description of the organization's mission, and the percentage of every contributed dollar spent on administration and fundraising. The organizations themselves provide this information; the LFCC checks the calculation.

To be eligible to receive funds, a charity must, at a minimum, have a health or welfare mission, submit audited financial statements, provide proof that it does not receive more than 80 percent of its funding from government sources, and give evidence that its administrative and fundraising expenses do not exceed 25 percent of revenue. When total administrative and fundraising expenses exceed 25 percent of revenue, the nonprofit must submit a plan to reduce them to 25 percent in the next fiscal year. Also, to be eligible, local charities must document "a substantial local presence in the local campaign area" (Chicago Area Combined Federal Campaign, 2002).

Application is free to participating nonprofits, except for an annual financial audit that most would pay for anyway. So, why doesn't every health or welfare charity in the United States participate? Perhaps they are unaware of how easy it is, or they do not expect to benefit because many participating charities receive no money. In the Chicago region, about 15 percent of participating charities in a given year receive no funds.

National campaign

OPM compiles data on local campaigns and makes them available on the Web. In this section, I summarize data on campaigns conducted from 1995 to 2001. In 2001, combined CFC contributions totaled $241.5 million, capping a period of uninterrupted growth stretching back to 1995 when it raised $189 million, an average increase of 4 percent per year. Because of budget cutbacks, it is not surprising that the number of employees solicited fell 3 percent from 4.0 million to 3.9 million. The more rapid 15 percent decline in number of contributors, from 1.7 million to 1.5 million, is harder to explain. We do know that increasing gift size drove revenue growth: in 1995, the average gift was $110, but by 2001 it had risen to $168, an average annual increase of 8 percent per year.

Payroll deduction generated the overwhelming majority of revenue, ranging from a low of 89 percent in 1996 to a high of 92 percent in 1997. The proportion of employees using payroll deduction ranged from 74 percent in 1996 to 78 percent in 2000. Payroll deduction, which helps people manage their cash flow, appears to increase the size of an average gift. In 1995, employees using payroll deduction contributed an average of $137 compared with $28 for other employee contributors. In 2001, employees using payroll deduction contributed an average of $199 compared with $62 for other employee contributors. The ratio of average gift made through payroll deduction to the average of other gifts fell from 4.9 to 3.2.

Raising money in the workplace through payroll deductions should be cost-effective. All local CFC campaigns follow a standard format and conform to rigorously enforced rules. In general, standardization reduces costs, so CFC offers a glimpse into what are arguably the minimum costs necessary to do fundraising in general. Campaign costs as a percentage of revenue ranged from 7.7 percent in 1995 to 8.7 percent in 2001. However, the low figure was an aberration; typically, costs exceeded 8 percent of revenue and showed no discernible trend over time.

Does success depend on size? Of the variety of ways to measure an organization's size, CFC prefers to use total annual revenue. Every year, CFC recognizes exemplary local CFCs in size categories based on total revenue. One could also measure size by the number of employees solicited. Performance measures used by CFC are cost per dollar collected, participation (contributors divided by employees solicited), average gift size, and largest dollar increase. The CFC Web site displays the historic trend of the first measure: cost per dollar collected of all local campaigns combined on its Web site. Analysis of the trends reveals that costs rise at 95 percent of the rate of revenue increase. When I examined the relationship among local campaigns, I found no discernible relationship between cost per dollar of revenue and the number of employees solicited. (These calculations and those that follow in this section are based on regression analysis, a statistical technique that estimates the relationship between a variety of variables. I looked at data for the 2001 campaign from ninety-four randomly sampled campaigns out of the 376 local CFCs. I sampled every fourth campaign, starting with the second; campaigns are listed alphabetically by state but apparently randomly within state. No data were reported for two local CFCs in the sample, and only the campaign for overseas personnel was discarded as being completely atypical.) Although the results are mixed, it appears that larger campaigns are slightly more efficient than small ones, in the sense of raising more revenue per dollar.

Every year, CFC recognizes local campaigns that have the highest participation rates, average gift size, and largest dollar increase. Table 2.1 shows the summary results for the 2001 campaign. Small campaigns seem to do well relative to their peers, but appearances are deceptive because small campaigns vary considerably.

I do not have prior-year data for local campaigns, so I will examine the relationship between campaign size and, first, participation and, second, average gift. Participation rates vary considerably. The average in my sample was 30 percent, and the standard deviation was 0.13, meaning that about two-thirds of local campaigns had participation rates between 17 percent and 43 percent. There is no discernible relationship between number of employees solicited and participation rates. I detect a weak relationship between revenue raised and participation. Tripling the revenue raised increases the participation rate by about four percentage points. There is a stronger relationship between cost per employee and participation. Increasing cost per employee by $1 increases the participation by two percentage points.

Average gift size is also an important measure of performance. The sample average is $165, with a standard deviation of $61. Thus, two-thirds of local CFCs produced average gifts between $226 and $104. I can find no relationship between the number of employees solicited and average gift. There is a weak relationship

Table 2.1. Exemplary local campaigns by size

Campaign Size Categories, Based on Annual Revenues	Measures of Excellence		
	Highest Dollar Increase, %	Highest Participation Rates, %	Highest Average Gift, $
Over $2 million	33	67	347
$1 to $2 million	25	60	309
$250,000 to $1 million	27	92	359
Under $250,000	236	83	470

between the amount of revenue raised and average gift. Tripling the size of a campaign increased average gift size by about $6. These patterns are not inconsistent. If highly paid employees are concentrated in large urban areas (the big local CFCs), and if they prefer national and international charities, then we would expect average gifts to be larger in the campaigns that raise the most revenue. There is a strong relationship between campaign cost per employee solicited and the average gift. A minimal campaign generates an average gift around $90. Increasing the cost per employee by $10 increases the average gift by $130.

The evidence is mixed on whether campaign size matters to local charities. On the one hand, the proportion of total revenue going to local charities decreases as total revenue increases. On the other hand, the proportion of revenue going to local charities increases as the number of employees solicited (size) decreases. These patterns may not be inconsistent. Again, if we assume that highly paid employees are concentrated in large urban areas (the big local CFCs), and if they prefer national and international charities, then we would expect the proportion of total revenue going to local charities to decrease as total revenue increases. But if the number of employees solicited is a measure of campaign size, we speculate that federal employees in small communities are more likely to have personal contact with people who work for local charities, or who are helped by them, and the proportion of total revenue going to local charities is greater in areas with fewer employees.

It is interesting to observe that $7 million, or 3 percent, of donations is not designated to any specific charity. Undesignated gifts are distributed to charities in proportion to the designations of all other employees. By not designating their gift, donors are choosing, for practical purposes, to allocate their contribution among charities in proportion to the number of dollar "votes" the charities receive from their co-workers. It is understandable that people would defer to the "experts" at a United Way or other federated campaign, but it is not clear why they would put their dollars to a vote. There is not a lot of money at stake, but it is a curious fact for theorists of altruistic behavior to contemplate.

Chicago campaign

The Chicago Area CFC (CACFC) graciously gave me access to individual giving records, stripped of identifying personal information, for the period 1999 through 2001. The donor pool was fairly constant during this time period at slightly more than 61,000 individuals. We observed the same trends in giving in Chicago that we noted for the national campaign. There were 38,845 records for 1999, 37,333 for 2000, and 35,824 for 2001. A "record" is defined as a gift by one employee designated for one organization. When an employee designates multiple organizations, he or she generates one record for every organization designated.

The 8 percent decline in the number of records in this period primarily reflects fewer donors. In 1999, the number of donors was 23,493, and there were 15,352 multiple designations. By 2001, the number of donors had dropped to 20,613, but multiple designations barely slipped to 15,211. Either the people who dropped out of the group of givers did not designate multiple organizations, or the popularity of multiple designations increased among the remaining givers, which seems more likely.

Paralleling the national trend, the average gift in the CACFC increased from $113 in 1999 to $128 in 2001. The largest gift in 1999 and 2001 was $3,900. Only one out of fifty gifts was $520 or higher, and only one in two hundred was more than $1,000. At the other extreme, 10 percent of gifts were less than $7 per year. These were probably lump-sum gifts, or gifts from people who worked less than a year, because the minimum deduction per pay period is $2 per month for military personnel and $1 per biweekly pay period for civilians. The most popular gift levels are given in Table 2.2. Designation amounts shown for both single pay periods and annual gifts account for two-thirds of all records. It is clear that workplace giving attracts many small donations; indeed, that is one of its virtues.

The first set of columns in the table shows number of designations by level per pay period. Although it is possible that employees might have authorized a payroll deduction of $2.50 per pay period, these employees more likely split a deduction of $5 between two

Table 2.2. Summary statistics for pay period and annual gifts, Chicago 2001 Combined Federal Campaign

	Single Pay Periods			Annual Gifts	
	Records	Gift Size, $		Records	Gift Size, $
	2,382	1.00		1,073	5.00
	2,754	2.00		1,114	10.00
	1,847	2.50		865	20.00
	1,117	3.00		1,137	50.00
	1,043	4.00		1,064	100.00
	6,217	5.00			
	2,879	10.00			
Totals	18,239			5,253	

charities equally. The second set of columns shows the popularity of various annual gift amounts. Many employees made one-time contributions.

Organizations assisted by CACFC

In 2001, the Chicago region's donor's guide filled 102 pages and listed 1,804 organizations. The discussion in this section is based on 2001 CACFC data. Strikingly, 281 organizations received no contributions, and another 228 received only one, which together comprise 28 percent of the organizations listed in the donor's guide. To maximize choice, even at the expense of higher administrative costs, there is no provision in federal regulations allowing deletion of an organization from the campaign for lack of donor interest. The most popular organization was the United Negro College Fund, which received 2,020 contributions. The second most popular was the American Red Cross with 1,344 contributions. The third most popular "organization" was "undesignated," which garnered 847 contributions.

The one hundred most popular charities (as measured by total gifts) were selected for the summary analysis in this section. An important question is whether donor choice disproportionately benefits local organizations. In the donor's guide, national and international organizations outnumber local ones by three to one, but among the top one hundred, thirty-seven were local organizations compared with forty-seven national or international.

The CACFC is extremely important to a handful of charities. One local charity that is popular with postal service employees derives 86 percent of its public support from this source alone. Two charities receive about one-third of their public support from CACFC, and two receive about one-fourth. By contrast, sixty-seven out of seventy-eight organizations receive less than 3 percent of their public support from CACFC.

Virtually every type of organization was represented in the top one hundred, although health-related organizations dominated. Of the seventy-six organizations that could be identified within broad categories, thirty-one were health related, twelve were human service agencies, twelve dealt with the environment or animal welfare, eight were international, six were public benefit, four were related to education, three were arts and cultural organizations, and three were religious in nature. At least one organization in each of the education, environment, animal welfare, human services, and health care categories was nothing more than a funding conduit, raising money and parceling it out to other charities. In some cases, the other charities were members; in other cases, funds were awarded competitively.

An intriguing piece of information that the donor's guide reports for each charity is total revenue divided by administrative and fundraising costs. The ratio is calculated by the charity and checked by CACFC staff, based on primary data taken from the charity's Internal Revenue Service Form 990 reports. The CFC interprets this number as the proportion of each contributed dollar siphoned away from program support—high is bad, low is good. It is beyond the scope of this chapter to critique the calculation and its interpretation. Suffice it to say, federal policy limits participation to charities with ratios that are 25 percent or less. If a charity exceeds this limit, it must submit a plan to reduce it to 25 percent or less within a reasonable time. The highest ratio among the top one hundred was 24.9 percent, whereas the lowest was 0.2 percent for a funding conduit. The average ratio was 11.1 percent.

Concluding thoughts

Payroll deduction is popular. It generates an enormous number of small gifts. CFC's average cost is generally below 9 percent of revenue. There is no discernible relationship between number of employees solicited and participation rates. I detect a weak relationship between revenue raised and participation. There is a stronger relationship between cost per employee and participation and between campaign cost per employee solicited and the average gift. The proportion of total revenue going to local charities decreases as total revenue increases, but the proportion of revenue going to local charities increases as the number of employees solicited (size) decreases.

Other conclusions are more elusive. Do rising incomes cause payroll deductions to lose popularity? Is there a minimum ratio of fundraising cost to revenue that could serve as a standard against which to measure efficiency of all fundraising? In deciding whether to give to a charity, do people care about administrative and fundraising costs? Researchers always call for more research, but practitioners need answers to these questions, too. These questions are ripe for future research on the role that the CFC plays both in the lives of federal workers and the future of local nonprofit organizations that participate in these campaigns.

References

Chicago Area Combined Federal Campaign. *Everyday Heroes: Donor Guide.* Chicago Area Combined Federal Campaign, 2002.

Chicago Area Combined Federal Campaign. "Charitable Fundraising Within the Federal Service." [http://www.opm.gov/cfc/html/cfc_hist.htm]. July 2003.

National Committee for Responsive Philanthropy. *Workplace Fund Raising: A Primer.* Washington, D.C.: National Center for Responsive Philanthropy, 1997.

WOODS BOWMAN *is associate professor of public service management at DePaul University in Chicago, IL.*

Much of what donors and regulators know about nonprofit organizations comes from public financial statements. Do charities track and report their expenses correctly?

3

Current practices in allocation of fundraising expenditures

Mark A. Hager

NONPROFIT COST ACCOUNTING practices invite organizations to place or divide expenditures among three functional categories. These functional categories are program expenses, which relate to the services and activities of nonprofits; fundraising expenses, which relate to efforts to raise contributions; and management and general expenses, which relate to the administrative functions of the organization. To comply with generally accepted accounting practices (GAAP), nonprofit accountants, treasurers, and consultants tag expenses as one or another of these functional expenses.

The job of tagging and tallying functional expenses is complicated by the fact that some items and tasks span two or all three categories. For example, an organization may have one total for the paper, toner, electricity, and repairs associated with the copying machine. However, because the copying machine is probably used for program, administrative, and fundraising purposes, the copier costs should be divided in some reasonable way among these three functions. Another example is staff time for people who wear several hats. If an executive director is involved in service delivery,

NEW DIRECTIONS FOR PHILANTHROPIC FUNDRAISING, NO. 41, FALL 2003 © WILEY PERIODICALS, INC.

administration, and fundraising, then her salary expenses should be proportionally divided and reported among these categories. Accountants have a technical term to describe the division of discrete expenses among several functional categories: allocation. Allocation of expenses across functional categories is a means of most accurately representing the total program, administrative, and fundraising expenditures of a nonprofit organization.

Correct allocation of costs to functional categories is important for three reasons. First, nonprofit managers need accurate information about how they are spending their money and how much different activities cost. Because staff salaries are a large portion of expenses for many nonprofit organizations, accounting for time spent on different functional tasks is critical. Executive management teams and boards of directors rely on this information to help plan the strategic future of their organizations. If financial accounting decisions generate bad information, managers may end up making bad decisions. Knowing how much money is spent on fundraising, administration, and programs is an important dimension of responsible management.

Second, research and policy professionals are making strides in mapping and understanding a growing nonprofit sector. Financial documents carry great weight in assessing the scope and dimensions of this sector. If inaccuracies creep in, the resulting picture carries those same inaccuracies. This problem hampers efforts to benchmark nonprofit financial characteristics as well as public policy efforts that rely on objective research.

Third, donors may be misled. Accurate accounting, especially the accurate allocation of functional expenses, matters because financial documents are a primary means by which donors assess whether a particular organization is a worthy recipient of contributions. Although the practice of assessing charities based on their spending in different functional categories (programs, fundraising, administration) is questionable, it is becoming firmly entrenched in the ratings and rankings generated by watchdogs, federated fundraisers, the popular media, researchers, donor-advised funds, foundations, and others with a stake in comparing charities against each other.

Sometimes charities have good reasons to make themselves look a particular way to their publics, even if it means that their accounting is not up to GAAP. In this chapter, I present a brief overview of the current practice of fundraising expense allocation, particularly regarding professional fundraising fees and the treatment of joint education-fundraising appeals. The chapter is presented in four sections. First, I note several resources that shape and guide current accounting policies regarding allocation. Second, I report on how nonprofit organizations are currently reporting professional fundraising fees on Form 990, the annual report required of most charities by the Internal Revenue Service. Third, I discuss the responses to several questions on the allocation of fundraising expenses asked on a recent survey of nonprofit organizations. Fourth, I provide a few concluding observations on the current practices of expense allocation by nonprofit organizations in the United States.

Where to look for the rules

Because most nonprofit organizations file Form 990 each year, and because Form 990 requires nonprofits to report all expenses in the three functional categories described above, most nonprofits have come face to face with the requirements and challenges of expense allocation. The Form 990 instructions, mailed each year to most U.S. charities, give some guidance on allocation. The instructions for Part II say that a "reasonable method of allocation may be used" and that the method of allocation should be documented in the organization's records. The instructions also give additional guidance on allocation of indirect expenses and the treatment of "joint cost" expenses. Form 990 instructions are a primary point of reference for most nonprofits when the topic of expense allocations arises.

However, some organizations need more guidance, and a variety of printed resources are available that spell out allocation issues in clear language. Accountants and policymakers have spent a lot of time thinking and writing about this issue. Two places to turn are the American Institute of Certified Public Accountants' (AICPA) *Audit and Accounting Guide for Not-for-Profit Organizations* (2003) and *Not-For-Profit GAAP,* (Larkin and DiTommaso, 2003). Both of these guides give clear explanations and examples for the rules laid out by the Financial Accounting Standards Board, the division of the Financial Accounting Foundation that outlines accounting principles for for-profit and nonprofit organizations. The Financial Accounting Standards Board (1993) issued its statement number 117, which provided a number of guidelines on nonprofit financial accounting, including the allocation of functional expenses. Another guiding document is Circular A-122 (see also A-21 on educational institutions) and its attachments, compiled by the federal Office of Management and Budget (1998). A-122 governs cost principles for nonprofit organizations that receive federal government grants and contracts.

These five resources also discuss a specific issue of cost allocation that is popularly referred to as joint cost allocation. Although any cost that spans functional categories is sometimes referred to as a joint cost, joint cost allocation has come to refer specifically to fundraising appeals that share space with program or administrative content. An example is a mailed flyer that describes the warning signs of breast cancer *and* makes an appeal for contributions to an organization with a mission of fighting breast cancer. The warning signs, as educational material, might legitimately be thought of as a program expense. The appeal, however, cannot legitimately be thought of as anything other than fundraising. Because many nonprofits feel pressure to minimize allocations to fundraising, some use the educational content as an excuse to account for the entire flyer as a program expense. This practice became common enough to catch the attention of policymakers and regulators.

The rules that govern fair allocation of joint costs as fundraising expenses are currently governed by one main document. Whereas the joint cost rules have applied to some kinds of nonprofit organizations since the late 1970s, the AICPA "Statement of Position 98–2" clarified and applied the rules to all public charities in 1998.

According to the statement, expenses of joint cost appeals must be tagged as fundraising unless they pass a series of tests that allow for allocation of part of the expenses to programs or administration. The rules are technical, however, and nonprofits, accountants, and policymakers have wondered how well and how often the rules are applied. Rules on joint cost allocation, like all rules of allocation, are good only if they are followed consistently by the charities to which they apply.

Form 990: Allocation of professional fundraising expenses

Public charities with gross receipts of at least $25,000 in any given year are required by the IRS to file Form 990. This form is the only documentation of nonprofit finances that is publicly available. Consequently, the information in Form 990 provides the basis for benchmarks and watchdog standards on nonprofit financial performance. Proper benchmarks and proper evaluation of individual charities presupposes that the information provided in Form 990 is accurate, including an accurate allocation of joint cost and other expenses. However, observers have noted a high number of nonprofits that report substantial contributions and no associated fundraising costs. Although some organizations might legitimately report zero fundraising costs, the answer for many lies in misrepresentation of expenses or a lack of understanding about cost accounting rules regarding allocation of expenses. This concern underlies the investigations in the remainder of this chapter.

The statement of functional expenses is in Part II of Form 990, which is page two of the main form. In this part, nonprofits are asked to report program services, management-general, and fundraising expenses for eighteen different categories, with five extra lines for itemizing other expenses. Examples of expense lines are salaries and wages, supplies, printing and publications, and travel.

The line that most explicitly relates to fundraising is line 30, professional fundraising fees. (See Exhibit 3.1.) The instructions

Exhibit 3.1.   Form 990, parts II and III.

Form 990 (2002)   Page **2**

Part II **Statement of Functional Expenses**   All organizations must complete column (A). Columns (B), (C), and (D) are required for section 501(c)(3) and (4) organizations and section 4947(a)(1) nonexempt charitable trusts but optional for others. (See page 21 of the instructions.)

Do not include amounts reported on line 6b, 8b, 9b, 10b, or 16 of Part I.		(A) Total	(B) Program services	(C) Management and general	(D) Fundraising
22	Grants and allocations (attach schedule) . . (cash $ _____ noncash $ _____)	22			
23	Specific assistance to individuals (attach schedule)	23			
24	Benefits paid to or for members (attach schedule)	24			
25	Compensation of officers, directors, etc. . .	25			
26	Other salaries and wages	26			
27	Pension plan contributions	27			
28	Other employee benefits	28			
29	Payroll taxes	29			
30	Professional fundraising fees	30			
31	Accounting fees	31			
32	Legal fees	32			
33	Supplies	33			
34	Telephone	34			
35	Postage and shipping	35			
36	Occupancy	36			
37	Equipment rental and maintenance	37			
38	Printing and publications	38			
39	Travel	39			
40	Conferences, conventions, and meetings . .	40			
41	Interest	41			
42	Depreciation, depletion, etc. (attach schedule)	42			
43	Other expenses not covered above (itemize): **a**	43a			
b	....	43b			
c	....	43c			
d	....	43d			
e	....	43e			
44	Total functional expenses (add lines 22 through 43). *Organizations completing columns (B)-(D), carry these totals to lines 13–15* .	44			

Joint Costs. Check ► ☐ if you are following SOP 98-2.
Are any joint costs from a combined educational campaign and fundraising solicitation reported in **(B)** Program services? . ► ☐ Yes ☐ No
If "Yes," enter **(i)** the aggregate amount of these joint costs $_____; **(ii)** the amount allocated to Program services $_____;
(iii) the amount allocated to Management and general $_____ ; and **(iv)** the amount allocated to Fundraising $_____

Part III **Statement of Program Service Accomplishments** (See page 24 of the instructions.)

What is the organization's primary exempt purpose? ►...

All organizations must describe their exempt purpose achievements in a clear and concise manner. State the number of clients served, publications issued, etc. Discuss achievements that are not measurable. (Section 501(c)(3) and (4) organizations and 4947(a)(1) nonexempt charitable trusts must also enter the amount of grants and allocations to others.)

Program Service Expenses
(Required for 501(c)(3) and (4) orgs., and 4947(a)(1) trusts; but optional for others.)

a ....
....
.... (Grants and allocations $)

b ....
....
.... (Grants and allocations $)

c ....
....
.... (Grants and allocations $)

d ....
....
.... (Grants and allocations $)

e Other program services (attach schedule)   (Grants and allocations $)

f Total of Program Service Expenses (should equal line 44, column (B), Program services) . . . . . ►

Form **990** (2002)

Internal Revenue Service, 2000, p. 2.

specify that nonprofits should enter on this line their fees paid to outside fundraisers who are paid primarily for solicitation campaigns they conducted or for consultation services connected with a solicitation of contributions by the organization itself. Given these instructions, it is hard to imagine how an organization could think of these expenses as anything other than fundraising. Indeed, before 1997, Form 990 "blacked out" the program services and management-general expenses options, constraining nonprofits to report professional fundraising fees only as a fundraising expense. However, this constraint was removed in the 1997 form. Following a recommendation from the National Association of State Charity Officials' Quality Reporting Task Force, the IRS allowed for allocation of professional fundraiser fees to program services and management-general.

An evaluation of whether this decision was a good one can be made from a focus on current practices of cost allocation on line 30. Consequently, I reviewed Form 990 information in the NCCS-GuideStar National Nonprofit Research Database (FY2000), housed at the National Center for Charitable Statistics at the Urban Institute in Washington, D.C. I was able to include just over 180,000 public charities that filed Form 990 in 2000. I learned that only about one-third of nonprofits (34 percent) report any fundraising expenses on their 2000 Form 990. Only 5 percent of nonprofits, just over nine thousand organizations, report professional fundraising fees.

How do these nine thousand organizations report these fees across functional categories? Two-thirds (67 percent) fully account for professional fundraising fees as a fundraising expense. However, a little more than one-quarter (26 percent) report *none* of these fees as fundraising expenses, instead reporting them as programs, management-general, or an allocation between these two categories. The remaining seven percent allocate some of the professional fundraising fees to fundraising but also allocate portions to programs or management-general.

If an organization has a legitimate cause to account for professional fundraising fees as something other than fundraising, these causes are probably rare, certainly less than a quarter of nonprofits that engage professional fundraising firms. Although the decision to allow nonprofit organizations to allocate professional fundraising fees to programs and management-general was no doubt made to improve the accuracy of reporting, this policy has almost certainly had the opposite effect. In the fourth year after allowing nonprofits to report these fees as something other than fundraising, a substantial minority of organizations is improving their illusion of fundraising efficiency by hiding these costs in the non-fundraising categories of functional expenses.

Further explorations from a national survey of nonprofits

These kinds of observations of the reporting of fundraising expenses on Form 990 spurred further investigation of these issues in a national study of nonprofit financial reporting. The "overhead cost study" received 1,540 survey responses from U.S. nonprofit organizations in the fall of 2001 and winter of 2002.

Although fees to professional solicitors and consultation services are combined in line 30 of Form 990, my colleagues and I asked about them separately in the overhead cost study. First, we asked organizations if they had contracted with a professional fundraiser in the most recently completed fiscal year. We defined a professional fundraiser as a person or firm outside of the organization who is paid to actively solicit gifts, including professional or commercial solicitors. Eight percent of respondents answered yes to this question, higher than the 5 percent of nonprofits that reported professional fundraising *or* counsel fees on Form 990 in 2000.

We also asked how organizations report professional fees or commissions on their financial statements. We gave options of fundraising, general or administrative, and program expense and invited respondents to check as many as applied. Because financial statements do not always rely on the same functional categories advocated by GAAP, we also included an "other" category and asked respondents to specify the nature of this category. Several organizations did not answer this question, so the results in Table 3.1 represent the 7 percent of respondents who say they contracted with a professional fundraiser and opted to tell us how they report the expenses.

More than half of the organizations in the study reported professional fundraiser fees exclusively as a fundraising expense. Con-

Table 3.1. How the 7 percent of U.S. charities report their professional fundraiser expenses

Expenses	Percentage
Fundraising only	55
Management or general only	15
Program services only	4
Other only	11
Fundraising and management or general	5
Fundraising and program	2
Fundraising and other	2
Management or general and program	3
Fundraising, management or general, and program	2
Fundraising, program, and other	1

sistent with the findings from the Forms 990, however, a substantial minority reports these fees purely as administrative or program expenses. A substantial number opted out of these functional categories, noting that they categorize professional fundraiser fees as advertising expenses or professional or consultant fees.

Fifteen percent of respondents allocate professional fundraiser fees across multiple categories. In all but 3 percent of cases, one of these categories is fundraising. Given the differences between Form 990 and survey responses, the results of the survey can possibly be thought of as how respondents *believe* their expenses should be classified rather than how they actually are classified. If this is the case, then a substantial number of nonprofits believe that professional fundraiser fees are a fundraising expense. However, given accounting rules and guidelines, a surprisingly high number consider at least a portion of these costs to be something other than fundraising.

In addition, we asked respondents if their organization had contracted with fundraising counsel in the most recently completed fiscal year, with fundraising counsel defined as a person or firm outside of the organization who is hired to advise specifically on fundraising. For this question, 10 percent of respondents answered affirmatively. We similarly asked this group how they report fundraising counsel expenses on their financial statements. Table 3.2 summarizes the responses.

The distribution of responses in Table 3.2 is similar to the distribution of responses for professional fundraiser fees in Table 3.1.

Table 3.2. How the 10 percent of U.S. charities report their professional fundraising counsel expenses

Expenses	Percentage
Fundraising only	51
Management or general only	21
Program services only	4
Other only	10
Fundraising and management or general	6
Fundraising and program	1
Fundraising and other	1
Management or general and program	3
Fundraising, management or general, and program	1
Fundraising, program, and other	1
Management or general, program, and other	1

One difference is that the percentage of organizations that think of fundraising counsel as a pure fundraising expense is a bit lower than the proportion that think of fundraising counsel this way, although the fundraising-only camp is still more than half of the relevant cases. The difference is mostly made up of organizations that think of fundraising counsel as purely an administrative expense, a group constituting one of five cases. The "other" category includes such labels as professional services and capital campaign expenses. Several indicated that fundraising counsel was donated or paid for by others.

Taken together, these two tables largely corroborate the results from the analysis of Forms 990. A substantial minority of nonprofit organizations are accounting for fundraising expenses as program services or administrative expenses, a practice that minimizes their reported fundraising expenses and maximizes their associated fundraising and program efficiency ratios.

As discussed above, a second functional expense item that is clearly tied up with fundraising is the allocation of joint costs. Form 990 asks organizations if they reported any program service expenses from any activities that combined an educational campaign with a fundraising solicitation. Less than 1 percent of filers of year 2000 Form 990 answered yes to this question, about a thousand nonprofit organizations in the entire country. In the overhead cost study, we asked our survey respondents if their organization combines educational campaigns (or other program activities) with fundraising activities. Over one-quarter of the nonprofits in the study say that they do. For those that answered yes to this question, we asked if their organization allocates portions of the costs to both programs and fundraising. One out of ten organizations was unsure, and just under four in ten say that they do not allocate joint costs across different functional categories. However, just more than half of organizations that say they combine program and fundraising activities also say that they allocate costs across categories of programs and fundraising. In raw numbers, more than 200 of the 1,540 respondents claim joint allocation of costs for fundraising activities that have a programmatic component.

Of course, the Form 990 findings and the survey findings cannot both be true. We know from Forms 990 that few organizations allocate the kinds of joint costs described in AICPA's "Statement of Position 98–2." We interpret the survey findings not so much as how organizations actually account for and allocate their costs but, rather, how they believe that their costs should be allocated given the circumstances of their organization. If this is a reasonable interpretation, then fewer organizations are accounting for joint costs than should be accounting for them. Consequently, contrary to the rules spelled out in "Statement of Position 98–2," many organizations are likely still using educational content in fundraising appeals as a means to account for such appeals as program services rather than fundraising expenses.

Conclusions

In this chapter, I point out two ways in which a substantial number of nonprofit organizations come up short on reporting fundraising expenses. Analysis of both Form 990 data and independent survey data reveals that professional fundraising fees are routinely tagged as non-fundraising expenditures. These data resources also suggest that joint costs between educational materials and fundraising appeals are not being documented as fundraising in the ways spelled out by current guiding documents. These findings, taken together with other findings regarding the accounting of functional expenses, suggest that America's nonprofit sector is weak on financial accounting. However, if issues of expense allocation do not enter into the daily trappings of most nonprofit organizations, perhaps they can be forgiven for it. After all, nonprofits have enough to think about, and most would rather spend their time focusing on the delivery of quality programs rather than arcane issues of accounting. Also, the rules do not always apply in obvious ways to some nonprofits, where fundraising, communications, education, and strategic planning often mix in the same processes. So, some organizations fail to invest in the details that would cause them to account for and report their transactions according to the letter of the law. Because the costs of misreporting are low, many nonprofits have little incentive to learn the rules that would bring their accounting practices into compliance with GAAP.

For some other nonprofits, though, fudging financial reports is likely due as much to strategy as to ignorance. Savvy nonprofits know that they are judged on how many of their total dollars they can put toward programs, and they know that donors want to believe that a minimum of their contributions is being used for administration and fundraising. So they find ways, some legitimate and some not, to represent as many of their expenses as programmatic expenses as they can. The social costs of such practices are low for most organizations, and the returns can be counted in accolades about efficiency and the dollars that such accolades bring in.

Whether the result of ignorance or strategy, the pervasive misstatement of fundraising costs sets impossible standards for all charities. If the average charity "officially" spends 75 percent of its annual dollars on programs, then honest charities find themselves possibly chasing a goal that they find to be impossible. Punished by donors, they either compromise on administrative costs or find ways to join their colleagues in reporting functional costs in ways that do not measure up to GAAP. They join a circular system that produces new benchmarks based on questionable accounting.

Although individual nonprofit organizations win in the short run, the bigger picture points to a variety of losers. As discussed in the introduction, expense allocation to functional categories is an opportunity for nonprofits to faithfully represent how money is spent in nonprofit organizations, an issue that has implications for managers, policymakers, and donors. When individual organizations consistently misaccount for expenses, managers get an unclear picture of the costs of programs and the costs of fundraising. Consequently, they run the risk of making choices about strategic direction that are not in the best interests of the organization. Policymakers, who rely on self-reports of nonprofit organizations, generate research that inherits all the flaws attached to the financial documents they study. Consequently, they run the risk of making public policy decisions that are not in the best interests of the nonprofit sector. Finally, donors make giving decisions based on the limited information they can garner on the efficiency and effectiveness of charities that seek their contributions. Although this creates a game wherein individual charities gain from illusions of financial efficiency, donors run the risk of putting their dollars to work in ways that are not in the best interests of their communities.

References

American Institute of Certified Public Accountants. *Statement of Position 98–2: Accounting for Expenses of Activities of Not-for-Profit Organizations and State and Local Entities that Include Fund Raising.* New York: AICPA, 1998.

American Institute of Certified Public Accountants. *AICPA Audit and Accounting Guide for Not-for-Profit Organizations.* New York: AICPA, 2003.

Financial Accounting Standards Board. *Statement of Financial Accounting Standards No. 117: Financial Statements of Not-for-Profit Organizations.* Norwalk, CT: FASB, 1993.

Internal Revenue Service. *Form 990: Return of Organizations Exempt from Income Tax.* Washington, D.C.: Department of the Treasury, 2000.

Larkin, R. F., and DiTommaso, M. (eds.). *Not-For-Profit GAAP.* New York: Wiley, 2003.

Office of Management and Budget. *Circular No. A-122: Cost Principles for Non-Profit Organizations.* Washington, D.C.: OMB, 1998.

Office of Management and Budget. *Circular No. A-21: Cost Principles for Educational Institutions.* Washington, D.C.: OMB, 2000.

Further Reading

Financial reporting is beginning to attract attention from a variety of nonprofits researchers. Several informative treatments of the topics discussed in this chapter are currently unpublished but available from their authors. Ranjani Krishnan, Michelle Yetman, and Robert Yetman explore the question of how some nonprofit organizations overreport program expenses on Form 990. Their article is titled "Financial Disclosure by Nonprofit Organizations" and is available from Robert Yetman (rjyetman@ucdavis.edu). Andrea Roberts (robertaf@mail1.bc.edu) provides a thorough discussion and analysis of joint cost reporting in "The Implications of Joint Cost Standards on Charity Reporting."

MARK A. HAGER *is a research associate in the Center on Nonprofits and Philanthropy at the Urban Institute, a social policy research organization in Washington, D.C.*

An increased focus on major, lasting human-improvement results and their prices may help to generate significant increases in value for service recipients and society. This chapter presents a vision and a case for pricing selected human-improvement results, and describes methods that may allow these prices to be developed.

4

Using prices to help obtain human-improvement results

Terrence R. Colvin

[A]ltruism is scarce; there is never enough to go around. The function of economics is to devise social institutions that make it possible to economize on altruism and still live tolerably. Competitive markets, *when they function well*, are such an institution.
—Solow, 1998, pp. 3–4

USING PRICES to help determine which human service results are obtained, how they get produced, and who receives them should be beneficial to both human service delivery mechanisms and donors that support them. (As Samuelson [1958] states, "Any society . . .

Note: The Advisory Board of the Center for the Study of Voluntary Organizations and Service in the Public Policy School at Georgetown University, a seminar at the Urban Institute (both in Washington, D.C.), and Virginia Hodgkinson, Mark Hager, and Michael Barzelay provided helpful discussions regarding the work reported here.

NEW DIRECTIONS FOR PHILANTHROPIC FUNDRAISING, NO. 41, FALL 2003 © WILEY PERIODICALS, INC.

must somehow meet three fundamental economic problems. (1) *What* commodities shall be produced and in what quantities? (2) *How* shall goods be produced? (3) For *Whom* are goods to be produced?" [pp. 15–16].) Price mechanisms, when applied appropriately, provide important resource allocation and other decision-making benefits in most domains. "The market economy provides a simple and effective method for determining the level of production of *private* goods: the price system. It provides incentives for firms to produce goods that are valued, and it provides a basis for allocating the goods that are produced among the various consumers. We often speak of the important role that prices play in conveying information: from consumers to producers, concerning the value they attach to different commodities, and from producers to consumers and from one producer to another, concerning the costs of production and the scarcity of these commodities" (Stiglitz, 1988, p. 146). Stiglitz also points out that "whenever private markets fail to provide a good or service, even though the cost of providing it is less than what individuals are willing to pay, there is a market failure we refer to as incomplete markets" (p. 76). Many good human-improvement results cannot be obtained as a private good from markets at competitive prices at present. If some of these results could be obtained from markets, market failure in these domains might be rectified. Because donors often want to see tangible results of their contributions, it seems reasonable to consider selected human-improvement outcomes as private goods, especially if an emphasis remains on human improvement—the ultimate goal. Some people feel that societies should try to acquire some of these results and services on a universal basis, regardless of what private donors do. If so, these results and services can also be seen as a public good. "[T]he limited supply of altruism can be saved up for those occasions when markets do not work well or for those others when markets do their job but still leave us with outcomes that 51 [percent] of us would like to improve, even at some personal cost to ourselves" (Solow, 1998, pp. 3–4). Governments can be donors and suppliers in the outcome-price approach.

Analysis framework

In this chapter, I examine the feasibility and utility of developing prices for some human-improvement results. I suggest procedures that should produce the desired prices. These procedures can be broken down into two groupings. The first group consists of information on benefits to recipients and to society and on costs and risks from outcome suppliers. Richmond, Mook, and Quarter (2003) provide a useful survey of alternative methods that can be used to calculate social benefits and costs of individual programs. Considerable controversy exists regarding the proper methods to calculate the values of nonmonetized social outputs. The information from the first group should assist donors and mechanisms of human service delivery to make their decisions regarding what they want and what they are willing to do under a variety of circumstances. Although valuable, activities in this group are not necessary. Markets work better when those doing transactions in it are well informed. Information in the first group can be produced by outcome producers, donors, or by third parties. The second group consists of procedures to get donors and outcome suppliers together and to establish prices for results, ideally in markets. (It seems useful to distinguish between an initial arms-length transaction between one supplier and one demander and a more typical market situation where there are several suppliers and demanders.)

Information development

First, price estimates require reasonably precise specifications of outcomes relative to what would have happened without intervention. Similar specifications are also needed for any milestone outputs that outcomes require.

The more widespread use of basic economics and business concepts and terms in the field of human-improvement philanthropy should facilitate improved analysis in it. Because I attempt to provide a demonstration of this in this chapter, it is important to clarify unusual meanings I attach to several of these concepts and terms.

In this chapter, *outcomes* are seen primarily as major, lasting human-improvement results. An illustration might be no recidivism for an ex-offender for five years from the time he leaves incarceration. I assume that each outcome consists of accomplishments for individual people and that outcomes for larger groups consist of the sums of individual outcomes. *Milestone outputs* are intermediate products that are useful for obtaining outcomes. An ex-offender staying off drugs for one year is an example. It is helpful to think of most human services as resource inputs that contribute to outcomes. Job or literacy training are examples of efforts that help people get higher incomes.

The distinction between final products, intermediate goods, and factors of production is helpful in many areas. It is useful to distinguish major human-improvement results that are of high value and long lasting from milestones that are important to getting these results and also from services that are helpful for their own sake. I expect that analysis of these distinctions will reveal opportunities to more clearly link services and milestone outputs to major outcomes. Such analysis should also help identify innovations that create value. Increased acquisitions of more lasting and valuable outcomes for needy individuals may create more value for them, donors, and society than the mix of outcomes, milestones, and services being acquired at present. This is especially the case if improved methods of focusing on, obtaining, and pricing outcomes can be developed. (After a friend challenged me to develop some analogies to other areas of life to show why I feel this way, I came up with the following questions: Do you spend money toward car purchases without finding out how many cars got bought or what they cost? When you want reliable transportation at a reasonable cost, do you buy steel, numerous steering wheels, and engines without having them assembled into cars and without asking their prices or that of the car? Can car manufacturers survive in competitive markets if 20 percent of their expenditures do not result in cars that pass minimal safety standards?)

For most goods, intermediate products and factors of production are desired only for their contributions to final products.

Demands for such goods are derived solely from these contributions. In the human results area, milestone outputs and resource inputs are often valued for their own sakes even if they do not result in major outcomes. For example, donors often value compassion for its own sake. Consequently, items that would be seen as inputs of labor or intermediate products in production processes in other domains can be valued as final goods in this setting. The proposed technique of having markets and prices for each of these items could be an effective way of addressing these properties.

The specifications for each result must include an explicit time frame for its accomplishment. This includes the times when the potential for accomplishment starts and stops and a time definition of lasting results. Other steps are also included in the first group. A service delivery mechanism must identify prospective recipients, and it should assess the values of outcomes, milestones, and services that may be offered to service recipients. Alternative estimates of benefits, including controversial ones, can be examined by donors who feel that these estimates help them make their decisions. In addition, the service mechanism should collect information on recipients' real desires for outcomes, milestones, and services. Next, suppliers should estimate the cash and total costs of producing the defined results, including the sum of the values of all resources *from all programs* used to obtain an outcome. Finally, the service mechanism should estimate its profits. The difference between prices and total costs is profits (or losses) for an outcome supplier. Ideally, the service mechanism would delineate outcome-attainment risks, assign risks to participants who will be taking them, and estimate costs of the risks. Finally, the service mechanism should identify places where proposed outcome determination and pricing procedures may do harm.

Price establishment and other actions

In the second set of procedures, donors decide what results and service inputs for what prospective recipients they are willing to fund at various prices. They also should decide what risks, if any, they are willing to take in obtaining the outcomes. Outcome suppliers must list the outcomes they are willing to supply at various prices, along with the risks they are willing to incur. In cases where both service mechanisms and donors agree on outcomes, recipients, risks, and prices, they can establish a price and enter into a transaction.

In addition to the two major groups of steps, many smaller actions are needed to make an outcome-price approach feasible. For example, total costs will generally need to be assigned to individual clients or service types. Standard cost-accounting techniques that allocate enterprise-wide indirect costs to individual projects should be used to do this. Program fundraising for suitable human improvements would focus on providing donors with clear information on which clients would get which specific benefits from donors' contributions. This would include information on who would take what outcome-accomplishment risks and at what costs. The service mechanism will need to do substantial work to specify, price, allocate, and explicitly manage risks. The service mechanism may offer financial incentives to clients and service suppliers to lower the risks of outcome attainment and to lower outcome costs, as discussed in the next section. Service providers may seek financing that is based on payments for outcome performance. The devil is in the details. (Many larger issues should be considered and addressed. Stiglitz [1994, p. 13] noted, "Among the broader set of questions are: How should these resource allocation decisions be made? Who should make these decisions? How can those who are responsible for making these decisions be induced to make the right decisions? How are they to know what and how much information to acquire before making the decisions?")

Activities and results

I have made several attempts to obtain or produce price information for several human-service results and to assess the value of this information. These attempts required work on defining specific outcomes that could be measured and, when obtained, documented. I also tried to obtain firm (fixed-price) side bids on supply and demand for outcomes that could be used in subsequent efforts to help establish markets. Efforts to ensure that a priced-outcome approach is used appropriately in the human service domain have been an important component of these attempts.

To date, my modest endeavors to uncover price information on human-improvement outcomes and milestone outputs from existing suppliers and donors have been unsuccessful. The outcomes I examined were not defined with the specificity that the approach championed here requires. Total costs that include overhead for outcomes, milestone outputs, and resource inputs have been difficult to obtain from individual service suppliers and from multiple programs that jointly produce outcomes. Credible program benefits and total cost documentation have not been available for the few programs I examined.

I made a serious attempt to identify precisely and define one specific outcome for a local program, to obtain quantified total cost and risk measures for it, and to obtain a firm, fixed (supply bid) price for it. In particular, I identified one urban program that seeks to produce successful lasting transitions from homelessness for Hispanic and refugee populations. I identified several methods to audit and document benefits at low cost, including the use of waiting lists to establish control groups and incentive contracts to reward clients for future reporting on their status.

I estimated the cash and total costs of the transitions, including the values of all resource inputs for other contributing programs. These included the costs of Americorps (a federal volunteer program) and program staff volunteers, the use values of working space, and the value of taxes not collected. From these, I developed a fixed-price offer to obtain future transition outcomes. This included an offer to return donors' financial contributions if specified results were not obtained by clients and verified by external audits within three to five years. The difference between this price and historical cash costs of obtaining outcomes is worthy of note. This calculation provides a quantified measure of the total risks that outcome suppliers believe exist.

The cash and total resource costs for the homelessness-reduction outcomes for this program were striking. They were much lower than I and several other observers expected. The production methods and client choices that cause these results are becoming clearer as I make comparisons with other programs.

In a second effort, I organized a study for a national program to define and quantify outcome benefits for clients and society. Increased income to clients was the principal outcome in this project. Clients and society obtained valuable outcomes at low cost. This was documented in such a way that financial and service volunteer donors could directly observe the financial rates of return their gifts provide and compare results from different programs. I estimated the financial rate of return for clients and society at about 3,300 percent over ten years. This return was principally created by the heavy use of volunteer resources in obtaining outcomes. About $500 in cash contributions resulted in clients earning, on average, $1,500 more per year for ten years, a total of $15,000. The study also estimated additional benefits to society. Excellent existing measures of milestone outputs were neither needed nor used. (Social accounting is a field that deals with items that do not have established dollar values and that are excluded from traditional financial accounting. The study referred to here needs to benefit from advances in this field. However, because the large majority of the benefits calculated consisted of items for which established financial values exist, the adjustments needed should be modest.)

Both of the service providers in the two endeavors just discussed were uncomfortable with raising funds using my benefit-per-cost results. One supplier feared that the compassion that motivated their program would be undercut if this approach were used. Both suppliers were concerned that emphasizing outcomes might undercut existing funding.

I have also worked on two experiments that are designed to lower costs of human-improvement outcomes and milestone outputs by allowing clients to "bid on the (outcome attainment) job." I am currently exploring the use of direct payments to certain ex-offenders for successful five-year nonrecidivism. This is being done to see if this practice might lower the total costs other methods have for obtaining similar results.

In another effort, paying financial incentives to clients for achieving milestone outputs that both they and program donors wanted lowered costs of obtaining final outcomes. Modest rewards to inner-city elementary and junior high students for getting good grades that they and their parents desired are associated with increasing grades from C to B levels.

I developed fundraising requests using an outcome-price approach for a literacy project in Central America and for the urban homelessness project described above. These requests employed a standard template used in financial markets to address private placement requests for funds. This template requires that risks be listed, roughly sized, and addressed with proposed management actions. It also requires that likely returns be outlined. Management qualifications and plans to ensure enterprise success are provided. In both cases where this template was used, clear specifications of anticipated program benefits and risks ensured that both could be managed.

Conjectures on opportunities

Championing and exploring outcome-price approaches in the human-improvement area has raised many intriguing ideas. (In addition to the ideas examined in this section, several others have been striking. For example, what would it take to estimate community-wide net benefits from the individual donor-to-recipient information that would be developed with the kinds of methods proposed in this chapter? What would it take to move from the individual-by-individual transactions examined here to communitywide or national-level scales of implementation?) One idea is that a variety of priced opportunities targeted to a variety of priced outcomes for different prospective recipients will be a useful component of the pricing of outcomes in selected situations. For example, one might pay $300 to give a child with specific personal and environmental difficulties an opportunity to graduate from her local public high school with a B average and offer $5,000 when this result is attained. Several prominent advocates of social justice have emphasized the provision of opportunities to disadvantaged people. (Some champion what I would see as the provision of resource inputs to provide opportunities. The priced opportunity-outcome pair suggested in this section offers an alternative.) For example, Rawls (1971) claims that "undeserved inequalities call for redress" to produce "genuine equality of opportunity" (p. 100). From these and other perspectives, a case can be made that the provision of a good opportunity can, itself, often be considered a valuable result. According to Sowell (1999), it is appropriate to add information on the costs of opportunities provided: "With justice, as with equality, the question is not whether more is better, but whether it is better at all costs. We need to consider what those who believe in the vision of cosmic justice seldom want to consider—the nature of those costs and how they change the very nature of justice itself" (p. 27). The approach discussed here adds cost information.

Fair, thoughtfully designed incentive payments to a person in difficulty should be a key component of a priced-opportunity or priced-result approach. Organizations in many fields share the financial and other benefits obtained from successful outcome attainment with those who can best affect results. In this example, the student might get a total of $2,000 when she reaches her goal, with $500 of this paid in progress payments for reaching milestones required to get there. This would mean that prospective recipients might usefully be considered as outcome suppliers along with other service providers. I wonder if increases in the *supply* of services provided to children in inner-city schools (many of whom appear not to want to be there) is the best use of additional resources to attain better results. Perhaps it is more effective to work on what it takes to get the children to *demand* better performance improvements. The example offered here might be best thought of as an action to help increase students' willingness and ability to obtain better outcomes.

Incentive-payment approaches may help determine what each party is willing to do to attain results. A service mechanism should obtain preferences of prospective recipients and donors for a variety of outcomes and the extents of their willingness and ability to obtain these outcomes. Prospective clients could get opportunities to show how serious they are about doing various things that may be useful in producing different outcomes. "In a society that places a high value on self-reliance, being the regular beneficiary of altruism may be dangerous to one's moral health. It can lead to unresisted dependency. . . . The object . . . should be to achieve a reasonable equilibrium between the norms of self-reliance and altruism" (Solow, 1998, pp. 3–4, 42). The techniques offered here may help achieve this goal.

This approach tends to transfer outcome-attainment risks. Methods of compensating risk takers for doing this successfully are used in other fields. Risks are best taken by those who are best positioned to manage and affect them. Clients and service mechanisms are better positioned to affect outcome attainments than donors. For instance, people training to be nurse practitioners and their trainers can address the risks of people not coming to work on time better than financial donors. On the other hand, insurance and enterprise financing in many domains is used to transfer certain risks that enterprises cannot control to other institutions that specialize in addressing them in competitive and cost-effective ways.

These steps might help prospective recipients to think through where they are headed and what they must do to get there. They might be empowerment devices to get clients' attention and put them more significantly in charge of their own destinies. Donors could get to see prospective recipients' estimates of what they are willing to do to obtain various results and what risks they are willing to take to get them before donors make giving decisions. In addition, donors should be given opportunities to fund results based on actual performance by clients as well as by clients' service suppliers.

Resources can be transferred from one person to another in ways that allow the preferences of the recipient to affect outcomes acquired by the recipient. These preference allowances range from all to nothing. Lump-sum transfers of financial resources to recipients empower them to do whatever they want. On the other hand, donors can give specific commodities to recipients if donors want to ignore recipients' preferences. In between, donors often subsidize the prices of specific goods or services, sometimes called "merit goods." In this merit-goods approach, donors allow recipients to choose goods they want by seeing how recipients allocate their own resources in light of the new prices they face. The priced-opportunity-priced-outcome idea examined here can be thought of as a variant of the merit-goods approach.

Significant increases in outcome success rates could result from fitting opportunity increases of the varieties just described. If recipients succeed in attaining results, reasonable increases in prices paid for these results relative to those paid for results that have significant attainment risks will probably be worthwhile. Opportunities offered that do not result in milestones or outcomes can have relatively low prices.

Conjectures on possible major changes

A second set of ideas is contained in statements of two different hypotheses regarding the sizes and kinds of results that outcome-price approaches could produce. These two hypotheses provide boundary estimates that can assist in assessing the methods discussed here.

First, consider a hypothesis that major changes will occur in the future because of applications of outcome-price methods. Multiple variants of this sort of hypothesis exist. At present, under this hypothesis, quantities of acquisition of major outcomes and milestones are fairly low in human-improvement domains where outcome-price methods are appropriate and their implicit prices are high. Implicit prices consist of the number of outcomes, milestones, and inputs provided divided into their appropriate shares of current total costs in situations where these calculations have not been done explicitly. If properly collected and analyzed, total costs could be reasonably allocated to each of the results and services provided. Olasky (1995) has argued that the ways Americans dealt with poverty, tragedy, and addiction before the welfare state were more effective than the current ways. His argument suggests that current implicit prices of results are high from a historical viewpoint.

In addition, many current services do not produce outcomes or major milestone outputs. Many people have social service needs, but service mechanisms suffer from scarcity of donated resources. Each suboptimally allocated resource has the opportunity cost of not providing needed services if the amounts of resources to be shared are limited. Consideration of the value that recipients and society get from priced outcomes relative to the value obtained from priced milestone outputs and inputs indicates that clients and society get more value from major outcomes than was previously realized. The creation of additional value seems to be a useful criterion for evaluating results in the public and in the private sector. For example, some leaders of the Kennedy School of Government at Harvard University have pointed out that creating public value in a variety of creative ways is a worthy goal for many institutions, including governments and not-for-profit and for-profit organizations (Moore, 1995). Donors may choose risk-adjusted objectives of total value creation and the use of investment-diversification allocations similar to those most of them use in their personal and professional financial lives. Weights for value creation for people in greatest need may be used in forming these objectives.

If creating public value is a worthy goal, then improved techniques to obtain valuable results at lower total costs are also worthy. Improved systems of calculation and organizational control, combined with improved information systems, are typically used to do this. Desired results are specified in such a way that "skimming the cream" in undesirable ways is not possible. Service suppliers who select and work with only the easiest cases receive lower payments than others who succeed with more difficult clients. More offers of opportunities get made to prospective recipients, including financial incentives when it is right to provide them. Under this approach, risks are identified and managed better than in the past. Limiting costs of services that do not create high value is also important. Changes occur in the acquired mix of outcomes, milestones, and services that do not produce results. The total value obtained for recipients and society rises significantly, even though this means rationing inputs that do not result in outcomes. Costs may also be lowered from fundraising efficiencies that outcome-price results may allow. As a result of these actions, outcome-supply curves shift downward and to the right, often significantly. The shifted supply curves intersect existing demand curves in places where they have significant price elasticity. Substantially more outcomes get obtained at substantially lower prices. As a result of this, donors like the results that can be produced at the new prices and contribute more resources to obtain them.

Conjectures on possible negligible changes

Finally, consider a hypothesis that little changes. In this case, outcome-price techniques do not create significant increases in value for needy clients or society relative to current approaches. This would mean that, all things considered, the current system is in rough equilibrium. Donors are satisfied with the mix of inputs, milestones, and outcomes they are funding at present. The number of outcomes, milestones, and services needy clients receive is about right, along with their distribution to groups of clients. The present mix of services and results creates the best total value for clients and society.

If this second hypothesis is correct, attempts to implement the outcome-price methods will provide sharpened definitions of outcomes. The development of explicit prices will add to our ability to identify equilibrium of needs and services, what it looks like, and the reasons why.

Summary

Outcome-price approaches deserve to be examined. Under certain circumstances, donors desire specific outcome results for individuals in need. For such cases, it seems valuable and practically possible to specify outcomes and to obtain and use prices for them and the milestone outputs needed to produce them. The approach must be flexible so that it can be adapted in appropriate ways in the human services domain. However, the benefits of this approach should be large enough to make this approach worthy of consideration by serious practitioners in the field of social service delivery.

The mode of analysis suggested here might be useful in framing strategic thinking and in suggesting avenues of innovation. The concepts, language, and issue framing provided by the outcome-price approach should be useful to serious workers in human services production and marketing. They should help identify and clarify problems and issues in areas where human-improvement results are desired, especially for decisions on program analysis and resource allocation. Pursuit of this approach should also provide important data, especially on prices and costs. As indicated by Solow (1998), "The need for relevant data is not just the peculiar craving of academic social scientists. It is the life-blood of rational social policy and its evaluation" (p. 43).

There are places where this approach should not be used. For example, there are many places where compassion is not best implemented by focusing on outcomes. Even if compassion is usefully expressed by outcome attainment, the methods championed here may need to be rejected if important risks cannot be balanced with the values of the approach. Taking significant risks of losses of human dignity for clients is probably one of these. However, for those cases where outcomes can be identified, priced, and balanced with risks, the approach has promise for funding a variety of social service delivery mechanisms.

References

Moore, M. *Creating Public Value: Strategic Management in Government.* Cambridge, Mass.: Harvard University Press, 1995.

Olasky, M. *The Tragedy of American Compassion.* New York: Free Press, 1995.

Rawls, J. *A Theory of Justice.* Cambridge, Mass.: Harvard University Press, 1971.

Richmond, B. J., Mook, L., and Quarter, J. "Social Accounting for Nonprofits: Two Models." *Nonprofit Management and Leadership,* 2003, *13*(4), 308–324.

Samuelson, P. A. *Economics: An Introductory Analysis.* 4th ed. New York: McGraw-Hill, 1958.

Solow, R. M. *Work and Welfare.* Princeton, N.J.: Princeton University Press, 1998.

Sowell, T. *The Quest for Cosmic Justice.* New York: Free Press, 1999.
Stiglitz, J. E. *Economics of the Public Sector.* New York: Norton, 1988.
Stiglitz, J. E. *Whither Socialism?* Cambridge, Mass.: MIT Press, 1994.

TERRENCE R. COLVIN *is president of Success Markets, Inc., and past chair of Synergy, Inc., a public policy contract research firm.*

Want to know how to milk the charitable sector of its lifeblood? Read on! This story tells you all you need to know to divert millions of dollars in contributions from America's charities.

5

Charitable fundraising for fun and profit: A satire

Bill Levis

CHARITABLE FUNDRAISING abusers siphon charitable contributions every day across the United States. This practice is a substantial part of the public credibility problems faced by the sector. Ill-intentioned fundraising activities are those activities that are conducted primarily, and often solely, for the financial benefit and personal gain of individuals and not for the public good. Efforts to uncover fundraising abuses have focused on the ratio of contributions to fundraising costs, but the use of this "fundraising ratio" has been ineffective in identifying and controlling fundraising abuses.

How might we eliminate fundraising abuses? One approach is to focus on provisions in the contracts between charities and independent fundraising contractors. These contracts for fundraising services are by law filed with state charity offices and available for public inspection, so a strategy for identifying and controlling fundraising abuse focused on ethical contract provisions could be implemented. First, ill-intentioned people are usually independent contractors and rarely on the boards or staffs of the charities involved. Second, they need to have written contracts to ensure that

NEW DIRECTIONS FOR PHILANTHROPIC FUNDRAISING, NO. 41, FALL 2003 © WILEY PERIODICALS, INC.

their intentions are achieved. Third, these ill-intentioned contracts contain unethical provisions or omit important ethical provisions. Such provisions are unethical, or unethical if omitted, according to the standards and codes of ethics of major national professional fundraising societies and trade associations.

Finally, the key unethical provision is co-ownership of the donor list where the ill-intentioned contractor is given absolute control over the charity's donor list. The Code of Ethical Principles of the Association of Fundraising Professionals (2002) states that "Members shall adhere to the principle that all donor and prospect information created by, or on behalf of, an organization is the property of that organization and shall not be transferred or utilized except on behalf of that organization" (p. 19). As the following satire illustrates, ill-intentioned fundraising contractors could not survive if this were a provision in their contracts. This satire is intended to contribute to a better understanding of fundraising abuse and potential avenues for identifying and controlling such abuse.

"Fun-and-Profit Fundraising Services"

The goal is to create a business that in ten years will produce $30 million in net profits annually through charitable fundraising activities. Despite its association with the nonprofit sector, contributing to the public good is not the goal and is not part of the business plan. The business could be called "Fun-&-Profit Fundraising Services" or simply "F&P." There are four keys to F&P's success:

Own a list of e-mail and mailing addresses for five million or more donors.

Keep data that distinguish donor acquisition from renewal results confidential so clients, regulators, watchdogs, reporters, and others can evaluate performance only on the basis of donor acquisition.

Hire the best direct-marketing talent and pay top salaries.

Have contracts that give F&P co-ownership and control over all
donor lists and complete control over expenditures, receipts, bank
accounts, and the number and content of e-mails and mailings.

The F&P goals can be achieved without breaking federal and
state laws governing charitable solicitations. Generally accepted
ethical standards will be adhered to as long as doing so does not
have a chilling effect on F&P net profits. F&P will operate solely
on a contingency basis, taking all the financial risks for its clients.
F&P clients will be pleased when F&P takes all the financial risks
and when the clients' gross income and the size of their donor lists
increase rapidly. They will be especially pleased when they see a
modest but immediate increase in their net contributed income,
even though F&P has counseled them that it will take several years
of substantial F&P investment before net contributed income
grows significantly.

F&P will charge clients at least $0.50 per e-mail sent and $1.00
per piece mailed in management fees, creative fees, production fees,
mark-ups, and quantity discounts. Once F&P's total annual volume
reaches ten million e-mails or pieces mailed, F&P will enjoy a net
profit of as much as $0.30 per e-mail and $0.60 per piece mailed.
That is a net profit of $2 million to $6 million, depending on the
mix. In ten years, F&P will be distributing 100 million e-mails or
pieces of mail annually and enjoying a net profit of $50 million.
Here is how F&P will get there.

Success factor no. 1: Own a list

The first key to success is for F&P to create and own outright an
"enhanced donor list" with e-mail and mailing addresses and lots of useful data. The idea is to identify from among 280 million people the several million Americans who like to give modest ($10 to $50) gifts to lots
of charities that pursue popular causes and who give several gifts per year
to the same charities. Over a period of years, the F&P enhanced donor list
will grow in number of names contained on the list and in the quantity
and usefulness of data for each name. In ten years, the enhanced donor list
will reach five million or more names with a comprehensive, highly
sophisticated donor profile for each individual.

When F&P has an enhanced donor list of five million names to which it e-mails and mails numerous fundraising appeals every year on behalf of ten to twenty charities, it will be big business, possibly the largest direct marketer in the nonprofit field. F&P will be extremely profitable because it will send out 100 million appeals annually and receive 10 million responses at an average of $30, for a gross income of $300 million in contributions. F&P will enjoy a net income of 25 percent of this gross income or $50 million (after recovering direct expenses and sharing a nominal amount with clients as necessary) and a net profit of 15 percent or $30 million.

The major front-end investment for F&P will be the costs associated with creating an initial enhanced donor list of several hundred thousand names. These start-up costs could be substantial. The time-consuming way to do this would be to enter into direct-marketing contracts with several charitable organizations. The main exception to a conventional contract will be a list ownership provision that allows F&P to add to its enhanced donor list the names, addresses, and other useful data for all of the client's donors. The objective is to create the initial F&P list and not to make money on the services provided. Charities will be selected that have popular causes and that will provide quality donors to the F&P list.

F&P will do anything necessary to win the initial contracts, including bidding low for contracts at a loss, covering all or a portion of the costs on a contingency basis, and paying staff or board members under the table. Of course, the fastest way to create an enhanced donor list would be to hire an industrial-espionage expert specializing in obtaining copies of computer data. Simply give the expert the names of charities with the best donor lists, and F&P will have its initial list in no time. The approach could be expensive, but it will save a lot of time.

Every year that F&P is in business, the F&P list will increase in size and quality. F&P will constantly add to and enhance the data on each individual's giving habits. F&P will record and maintain data on each gift to each of F&P's client charities. F&P will keep detailed records of the characteristics of giving for each name on the list, including the person's favorite causes, the best appeal strategy for each individual, the best timing for each individual, geographical considerations, and what that person does not like and will not give to. F&P will then target solicitations according to these characteristics.

F&P will send out dozens of solicitations yearly to each name on its enhanced donor list. F&P will do this for each of its ten to twenty active clients. Many individuals on the F&P enhanced donor list will receive hundreds of appeals annually from F&P clients. The strategy is simple: the more they give, the more often they will be solicited.

Once an initial enhanced donor list of 500,000 names has been created, F&P will be ready to market its list to charities. New charities will be added to the F&P client list every year. F&P may keep clients for only three to five years, dropping them as necessary to avoid scrutiny by the media or federal or state regulators. F&P will pick charities that are not well managed and, therefore, not likely to conduct an ongoing fundraising effort with their donor list once F&P has terminated its contract with them. They will also seek charities that are most likely to do a poor job of continued fundraising. The objective is to minimize the negative effects that competition from the fundraising efforts of former F&P clients might have on the appeals of F&P's current clients. F&P will encourage insiders (lawyers, accountants, and consultants) to set up bogus charities. But F&P will not use friends or relatives for this purpose because F&P will abandon sponsors of bogus charities if the situation gets out of hand with the regulators or the press.

Success factor no. 2: Keep data about donor acquisition and renewal confidential

The second key to F&P's success is to not have clients and others making the distinction between donor acquisition and donor renewal. Success factor no. 2 could also be called the "profitability factor." It is the key to being able to pocket the profits made through donor renewal while F&P clients, regulators, watchdogs, reporters, and others evaluate performance in terms of criteria for new donor acquisition. It is important for F&P to continuously counsel clients that it will take several years of substantial F&P investment before net contributed income grows significantly.

Having the F&P enhanced donor list will minimize F&P's losses with new donor acquisition. With its enhanced donor list and being the largest and the best at direct-response fundraising, F&P may even become efficient enough to make small amounts of money on some donor acquisition activities. However, the real profits are in donor renewal.

Many of the first donors acquired by an F&P client charity will make ten to twelve renewal gifts per year for the duration of the F&P contract. Ten gifts per year times five years equals fifty gifts, each ranging from $20 to $1,000. At 20 percent renewal costs, $800 of each $1,000 is gross income after deducting all direct expenses, all from a single average donor over five years. F&P expects to eventually have five million donors on its F&P list! And F&P will have up to ten active charity clients at any given time, and many donors will give $1,000 or more concurrently to several of those clients over five years. The 80 percent gross income from donor renewal, after deducting expenses, will be astronomical. That is where the profits are.

Of course, F&P passes some of this surplus onto the charities' clients, but just enough to keep them happy. If F&P gives the charities 10 percent of the 80 percent net renewal dollars, it will be only a small fraction of F&P's gross income. However, this sum is likely to be big bucks to the charities.

Success factor no. 3: Be the best

The third key to success is for F&P to be the most efficient and effective direct-response operation in the charitable fundraising field. F&P will hire or contract with the best direct-marketing talent and pay the highest salaries. They will hire the best direct-response strategists and managers, the best copywriters, the best e-mail and direct-mail list brokers, the best Internet and e-mail marketing services, the best computer analysts and services, and the best mailing services. F&P will buy at large-volume prices the best direct-marketing products and services. Although F&P will buy at the lowest possible price, charge clients at the highest possible price, and pocket any quantity discounts, F&P will not skimp on quality.

F&P will locate close to a U.S. postal facility or, better yet, get a U.S. Postal Service franchise of its own. F&P will hire the best lawyers to keep F&P out of trouble with federal and state charity regulators. F&P will hire the best accountants to keep the books and prepare general-purpose financial reports and Internal Revenue Service Forms 990 for its clients. F&P will have a department or employ a service dedicated to registering and reporting on behalf of F&P and all of its clients with federal and state regulatory offices and with the various charity-review groups. It will be extremely important to create the appearance of full cooperation with these oversight mechanisms, even and especially when F&P has no intention of changing its practices. Remember, F&P has no need to break any of the charitable solicitation laws to be highly profitable.

Success factor no. 4: Absolute-control contract

The fourth key to success is for F&P to have a standard fundraising service contract that contains all the provisions necessary for F&P to achieve its for-fun-and-profit goals and objectives. Such a contract will give F&P complete control over lists, expenditures, receipts, bank accounts, and the number and content of solicitations.

F&P will share list ownership even after the contract is over. F&P will also try to include all of the charities' donors acquired before the contract with F&P. F&P will have exclusive list rental rights but just for the duration of the contract. F&P will have a free hand to mail and e-mail to prospective and prior donors as often as F&P wants to use fundraising strategies and copy what F&P deems appropriate. F&P will have primary control over all receipts and bank accounts. F&P will have authority to deduct expenses and fees from the account. The client will not be able to withdraw funds from the account without F&P approval. F&P will require use of a lockbox service, preferably F&P's own lockbox operation. The F&P rationale is that such control is essential for accurate, complete, and timely data on results so that its managers can make informed decisions about subsequent solicitations. Control also allows for rapid reinvestment of receipts in additional fundraising efforts for the benefit of the client.

F&P will establish each client's overall direct-marketing operation as a separate cost center that disburses surpluses to the client only after all F&P expenses and fees have been paid and only after an adequate reserve has been accumulated to ensure coverage of future F&P expenses and fees. The contract provisions will avoid conflicts with industry practices and guidelines regarding list ownership and rental rights. At the end of a contract, F&P will always let the charity have a copy of its prior donors but with minimum data—that is, name, address, and last gift date and amount. F&P will not prohibit the charity from renting its list after the end of the contract. F&P will not give a former client any excuse to criticize or take legal action regarding list ownership.

To create the appearance of sharing list ownership during the contract, F&P will frequently remind clients that they will receive a copy of their donor list within ten days after completion or termination of the contract. It is better to discourage list rentals altogether during the contract period. If F&P wants to reap profits through rental of a client's list, F&P can rent the names under another list identifier without the client's knowledge. F&P will encourage list exchanges when F&P determines that use of the other list could enhance the F&P list. There is little profit in list exchanges, so the client will not be complaining about not receiving a share of the profit.

Other considerations

Above all else, F&P owners and staff cannot feel guilty about pressuring individuals on the enhanced donor list to give when F&P is pocketing most of the money. F&P will be providing millions of donors the pleasure of giving many times every year, and F&P will be doing society a great service by encouraging millions of individuals not only to give but to give often.

F&P will not try to comply with watchdog standards. Properly approached, these review groups will let the charity off the hook for two to four years of a major constituency-building campaign.

By that time, F&P will be planning to phase out. After three to five years, F&P may have gotten donors so angry at the charity that they will stop giving. However, donors will be angry only with the charity. These donors will not be angry with F&P because they will not know that F&P exists. Thus, donors will respond to another F&P client without making the connection back to F&P.

It is in F&P's best interest that charity regulators, watchdogs, and reporters continue to focus on the fundraising-cost percentage and related performance ratios, using the fundraising-cost ratio as the primary regulatory tool. It is also important to F&P that these same charity watchdogs continue to not distinguish between overseeing the performance of fundraising activities controlled by bona fide staff and volunteers and overseeing fundraising activities controlled by entrepreneurs such as F&P.

F&P will invest in misinformation activities to keep charity overseers focused on the fundraising cost percentage and related performance ratios. This will help F&P in several ways. Direct-mail and Internet fundraising is employed by many of the most prestigious national charitable organizations. They include leading hospitals, most voluntary health agencies, major religious groups, most advocacy groups, many social service organizations, and others. Most of those that are heavily dependent on their direct-mail and Internet activities have problems with higher-than-average fundraising-cost ratios. Because they are less skilled than F&P will be in direct marketing, their problems with fundraising ratios are more serious than any similar problems F&P might have. As long as charity overseers continue to focus on the fundraising-cost ratio, F&P can be assured that the prestigious, volunteer-run charities experiencing problems with the fundraising ratio will serve as a buffer between F&P and the oversight system.

Several credible expert witnesses are available for use in legal suits to invalidate the use of fundraising-cost ratios. Even the regulators and watchdog groups themselves have stated publicly that new organizations can spend 100 percent on fundraising in the early years of existence. Fortunately for F&P, federal and state regulators, charity watchdog groups, the accounting profession, the volunteer-run nonprofit mailers and e-mailers, and others are currently bogged down in a variety of accounting issues. Therefore, they are a long way away from trying to develop better regulatory tools for identifying and controlling the fundraising "irregularities" of entrepreneurs such as F&P.

F&P will also invest in misinformation and lobbying efforts to make certain that regulators, watchdog groups, accountants, and the press do not begin to look at list ownership, authority to mail and e-mail, control over receipts and bank accounts, and other aspects of F&P's fundraising service contracts. F&P will especially not want charity overseers to make a distinction between donor acquisition and donor renewal in their efforts to expose and control fundraising abuse. Whenever the press (with the help of regulators and charity watchdogs) begins to focus public attention on the reputation and credibility of one of F&P's clients, F&P will phase out the contract and move on to a new struggling charity that is not yet in the public eye.

Importance of being discreet

None of the recommendations outlined in this prospectus on charitable fundraising for fun and profit would be considered an abuse if only one recommendation were put into practice discreetly. For example, fundraising managers, consultants, and computer services have at times taken donor lists of employers or clients with them when they have moved on to new employers or clients. Used carefully and discreetly, such unethical (but not illegal) practices have usually not been discovered and therefore have not been a problem. Putting them all together provides a guaranteed formula for big-time profits.

However, following all of the guidelines at the same time as recommended here for F&P would surely annoy (if not anger) all the overseers and most of the leaders in the nonprofit sector if and when they find out. Therefore, it will be important for F&P to be as discreet as possible. But, being disliked, if it should happen, will be easy to live with when F&P is taking many hefty trips to the bank.

Moral

Taking advantage of people is easy. Discovering the professional fundraising firms with ill intentions is not easy. However, ferreting out these kinds of abuses is important for the nonprofit sector because firms that operate according to this model abscond with funds that are meant for the programs and operations of America's charities. When they are uncovered, the whole sector gets a black eye, not just the offenders.

The ubiquitous "fundraising ratio" has no role in solving this problem. Until regulators monitor the contracts between charities and ill-intentioned professional fundraising firms, these firms will continue to run unchecked amid the base of donors to charities in the United States.

Reference

Association of Fundraising Professionals. *Code of Ethical Principles and Standards of Professional Practice.* Alexandria, VA: AFP, 2002.

WILSON "BILL" LEVIS *is a senior associate in the Center on Nonprofits and Philanthropy at the Urban Institute in Washington, D.C.*

Professional fundraisers get a lot of bad press. This chapter documents the expenses, yields, and other characteristics of charitable telemarketing campaigns.

6

Cost-effectiveness of nonprofit telemarketing campaigns

Elizabeth K. Keating, Linda M. Parsons, Andrea Alston Roberts

CHARITABLE ORGANIZATIONS in the United States receive donations exceeding $240 billion annually. Seventy-six percent of these gifts are made by individual donors (AAFRC Trust for Philanthropy, 2003), which includes the response to fundraising solicitations. Nonprofit organizations may undertake fundraising efforts on their own or use professional solicitors to reach a wide audience of potential donors. Regardless of how nonprofit organizations conduct fundraising efforts, donors are entitled to know the extent to which their donations reach a nonprofit's beneficiaries.

Numerous studies demonstrate that donors want a significant portion of the amounts they contribute to benefit the cause for which the charity was established (Weisbrod and Dominguez, 1986; Greenlee and Brown, 1999; and Tinkelman, 1999). For example, the Better Business Bureau Wise Giving Alliance Donor Expectations Survey (Princeton Survey Research Associates, 2001) found that 79 percent of donors indicated that it was important to know the percentage of spending that goes to charitable programs.

NEW DIRECTIONS FOR PHILANTHROPIC FUNDRAISING, NO. 41, FALL 2003 © WILEY PERIODICALS, INC.

This concern has been long standing. A precursor to the Better Business Bureau's Wise Giving Alliance, National Charities Information Bureau, found that 82 percent of donors rated the amount spent for program important or very important in their decision to give (Glaser, 1994).

Given donor concerns about how nonprofits use their resources, accountability is an increasingly important issue for charitable organizations. Bradley, Jansen, and Silverman (2003) claim that the nonprofit sector could save as much as $100 billion annually if it operated more efficiently. Although the suggested efficiency improvements focus largely on the operating side, they estimate that one-fourth of the proposed savings could be realized through improvements in fundraising endeavors.

Our study examines a highly visible form of fundraising: telemarketing campaigns. Using data on individual telemarketing campaigns in New York State from the mid-1990s through the early 2000s, we examined the percentage of the total campaign proceeds available to support nonprofit programs. In addition, we investigated whether this percentage or "yield" is explained by environmental and organizational factors cited by the telemarketing industry. Finally, we explored whether pressure by one state attorney general (New York State's Eliot Spitzer) has translated into improved yields for nonprofits.

Motivations for outsourcing telemarketing campaigns

Fundraising campaigns that reach a large number of potential donors can be time consuming and complex. Campaigns of this nature are especially difficult for organizations with a small number of employees and volunteers. For these reasons, charities sometimes hire professional solicitation firms that have access to mailing or telephone lists and a larger, more experienced fundraising staff than the charity can employ (Hager, Rooney, and Pollak, 2002). The fee paid for professional solicitors' services can be fixed or determined based on the success of the campaign (for example, a percentage of the donations collected). The Association of Fundraising Professionals has a code of ethics that opposes commission-based arrangements. However, a number of fundraising firms have not adopted this code.

One presumed benefit of using professional fundraisers is that it allows the staff of the charitable organization to focus on providing program services. Professional fundraisers and charities also claim that these campaigns educate the public about a charity, its mission, and the issues it addresses (Suhrke, 2002). Hence, they argue that these campaigns may provide few direct donations but offer longer-term benefits through increased awareness or future gifts of time or money (Association of Fundraising Professionals, 2003a).

Monitoring and reporting on professional solicitors' practices

Although professional solicitors claim to provide benefits to nonprofit organizations, the service they provide can be expensive, and the uninvited phone calls may create ill will with the public. These factors, along with concern over the legitimacy of the charities and professional solicitors engaging in telemarketing, have led numerous states to increase scrutiny. For example, several states have imposed registration and reporting requirements on telemarketing campaigns. Some use these filings to create reports for the public detailing the financial performance of these campaigns. Our investigation indicates that at least fifteen state attorneys general offices issue annual reports designed to warn prospective donors about the inefficiency of telemarketing campaigns. Some states have attempted to protect donors by imposing limits on fundraising costs, but many of these limitations have been legally challenged and found to be unconstitutional (Strom, 2003).

The New York State report "Pennies for Charity" includes commentary and tables designed to highlight both the low average yields to nonprofits and the charities and telemarketers involved in particularly expensive campaigns. In 2001, New York

State Attorney General Spitzer proposed four reforms to regulate professional solicitors that request donations within his state. Spitzer supports taking legal action against some charities and professional telemarketers for fraud, making nonprofits obtain competing bids from solicitors before undertaking a campaign, limiting the tax deductibility of donations that do not eventually reach charities, and requiring professional fundraisers to disclose to donors their right to know how much fundraising costs (see the New York attorney general's Web site at http://www.oag.state. ny.us). He has subsequently been pressured to drop the requirement for competing bids from professional solicitors (Association of Fundraising Professionals, 2003b).

Illinois, with the support of forty-five other states and the federal government, sued a telemarketing firm for fraud, claiming that the fundraising firm misled potential donors about the portion of the funds it raised for VietNow that would directly benefit needy veterans (Greenhouse, 2003). The case, *Madigan v. Telemarketing Associates Inc.* (originally known as *Ryan v. Telemarketing Associates Inc.*), ultimately reached the U.S. Supreme Court. The fundraiser retained 85 percent of all donations it collected on behalf of the charity but represented to several donors that the charity would receive most of the funds collected. The Supreme Court unanimously decided that charging large fees for professional fundraising services does not constitute fraudulent behavior and that fundraising firms have no obligation to voluntarily disclose the cost of fundraising to potential donors. However, if potential donors ask about fundraising costs, solicitors cannot mislead donors about the amount of each donation available for programs (Lane, 2003).

The Association of Fundraising Professionals, in a friend-of-the-court brief filed in the recent *Madigan v. Telemarketing Associates Inc.*, argued that high fundraising costs associated with telemarketing campaigns are due to many factors besides the legitimacy or ethical standing of the nonprofit organization or the telemarketing firm involved (Association of Fundraising Professionals, 2003a). Such factors include the size of the campaign, the age of the charity, or the charitable cause involved. However, some watchdog agencies and state attorneys general are concerned that donors who respond to these campaigns are unaware of the large fees that some professional solicitation firms charge charities (Greenlee and Gordon, 1998).

Some insights from "Pennies for Charity"

We examined the New York State "Pennies for Charity" reports covering telemarketing campaigns carried out between 1994 and 2001. The report contains details of individual campaigns, including the charity and telemarketer, as well as the proceeds—both gross and net of the solicitor's costs. The data set contains a total of 4,778 campaigns carried out for 1,225 charities by 191 telemarketing firms (Table 6.1). Suhrke (2002) states that many factors, such as the type of solicitation and the expertise of the telemarketing firm, affect the amount of the collected funds that reach the charity. Our study investigates which organizational and environmental factors are associated with the ultimate yield from the telemarketing campaigns.

Question 1: How expensive are the services of professional solicitors?

Figure 6.1 depicts the distribution of reported yields. For 85 percent of all reported campaigns, the fundraisers retained a majority of funds. In fact, 1 percent of the campaigns reported to New York State that no funds were provided to the nonprofit, and in 3 percent of the cases, the campaign actually cost the nonprofit money (in other words, the fees exceeded the donations generated). Another striking insight is the low variance in yield. Just over one-quarter of all campaigns yielded between $0.20 and $0.30 to the nonprofit for each dollar raised. So, for the median campaign reported in New York State from 1994 through 2001, professional fundraisers retained $0.73 for each dollar in donations they collected on behalf of charitable entities.

Some campaigns had not collected all pledged amounts by the deadline for reporting to the state of New York. In case the inclusion of these campaigns had biased our results, we conducted two

Table 6.1. Purported charity focus

Charity Focus	Number of Campaigns	Percentage of Campaigns	Number of Charities	Number of Fundraising Firms	Average Gross Amount of Funds Raised, $	Median Yield, %
Abortion-related	110	2.3	17	20	633,556	45.5[a]
Activist or advocacy	422	8.8	76	51	634,568	31.1
Animal	62	1.3	19	18	170,644	29.4
Art	283	5.9	80	63	267,399	39.5[a]
Child welfare	303	6.3	66	64	722,182	20.0[b]
Civic clubs	363	7.6	99	51	111,054	25.0
Disabled	168	3.5	29	40	317,497	20.0[b]
Domestic assist	144	3.0	45	43	864,052	25.3
Emergency	101	2.1	31	29	112,210	26.6
Environment	301	6.3	50	38	330,961	35.7[a]
Fire	291	6.1	113	50	89,233	25.0
Gay and lesbian	15	0.3	6	4	248,580	53.0[a]
Illness	346	7.2	79	57	434,538	23.3
International	161	3.4	36	37	964,490	25.8
Military	358	7.5	107	46	215,283	23.0
Parent or family	64	1.3	16	20	460,490	33.9
Police	1,543	32.3	368	81	143,388	27.1
Religious	114	2.4	37	29	441,771	30.0
Retired	20	0.4	5	8	166,346	20.0[b]
School	315	6.6	76	44	247,765	49.6[a]
Sports	152	3.2	33	39	269,402	25.0
TV and radio	111	2.3	21	21	321,479	51.5[a]
Women	48	1.0	13	13	393,796	36.7[a]
Unclassified	185	3.9	91	61	254,738	25.0

[a]The yield is substantially higher than the median yield on the remaining campaigns.
[b]The yield is substantially lower than the median yield on the remaining campaigns.

Figure 6.1. Yield analysis

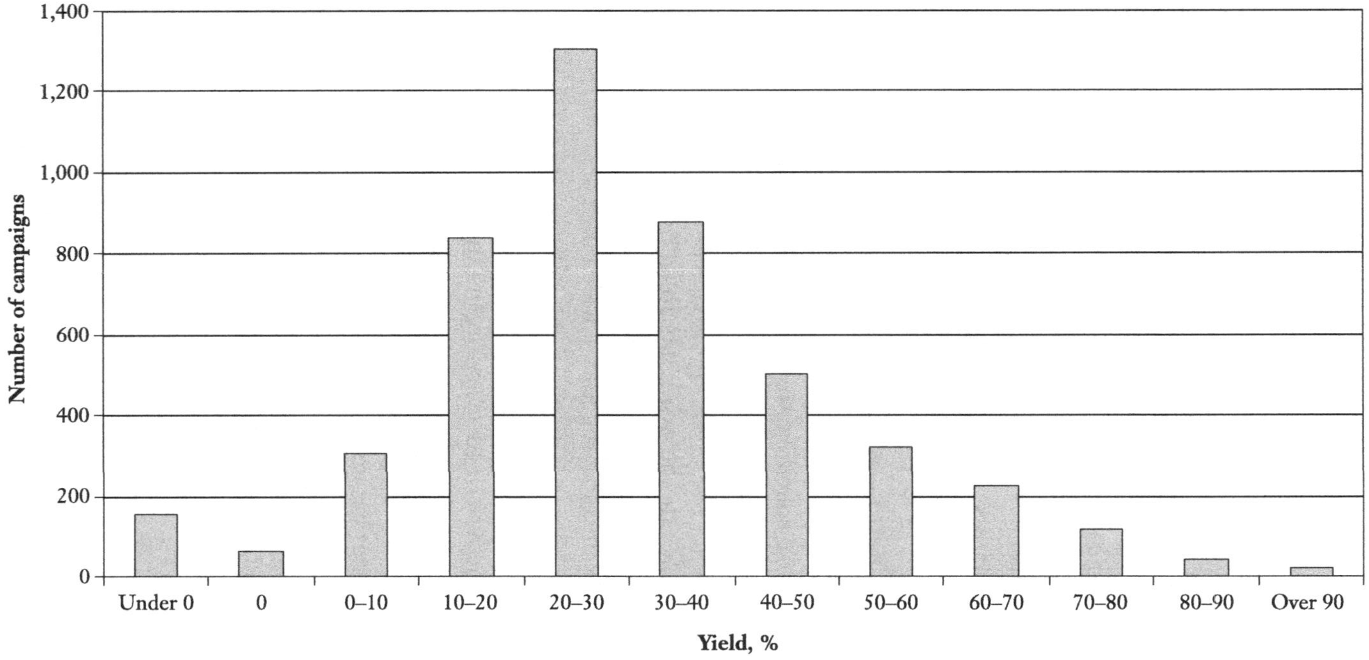

additional tests. If only fully completed campaigns were examined, then the professional solicitors still kept $0.73 of each dollar. If we assumed the most favorable situation—that all uncollected proceeds were collected and given to the charity rather than the solicitor—then the fundraising yield improved, with the fundraising firm retaining only $0.68 of each dollar raised.

We explored whether any telemarketers consistently paid half or more of the proceeds to the charity. Of the 191 telemarketers, only twenty-eight firms gave the associated nonprofits most of the proceeds in half or more of the campaigns conducted. Of these twenty-eight solicitors, only fifteen firms were active, conducting five or more campaigns during the period from 1994 through 2001.

Question 2: What type of nonprofits hire professional fundraisers?

Professional solicitors provide services to a wide range of charitable organizations (see Table 6.1). Based on the name, we classified the charities into twenty-four overlapping categories. If a nonprofit were to include the words "disabled" and "veteran" in its name, then it would be included in both the disabled and military categories. As the table suggests, a wide range of charities hire professional fundraisers. About one-third of campaigns are conducted for nonprofit organizations whose names suggest that they are police-related. Activist or advocacy organizations, civic clubs, groups that support the military, and illness-related associations together represent another one-third of the campaigns.

As Spitzer has indicated, organizations may select a name that is misleading or similar to a better-known charity to solicit funds. We were unable to determine which organizations fell into this category; hence, Table 6.1 should be interpreted as depicting the "purported" rather than actual focus of a charity.

Question 3: Is the yield related to the charity's purported focus?

As Table 6.1 indicates, the median yield paid to charitable organizations was related to the purported industry focus. In particular, gay and lesbian-oriented organizations, TV and radio stations, school-affiliated charities, and abortion-related organizations (both "pro-life" and "pro-choice") received yields of 46 percent to 53 percent, in contrast to the median yield of 27 percent. Organizations related to retirement, disability, and child welfare received a yield of 20 percent, which is substantially lower than the median yield on all campaigns.

Question 4: Is the yield related to the type of telemarketing solicitation?

Telemarketing campaigns varied as to the type of solicitation being conducted. As Suhrke (2002) describes, some solicitations involve the sale of tickets to a special event, such as a performance, or sale of advertisements to be contained in a publication, for example, a yearbook. Either of these forms of solicitations may be more costly than a request for a donation because the "contribution" includes the cost of the event or advertisement. New York State, however, does not ask for the type of solicitation to be disclosed. To determine if the costs varied by type, we classified the campaigns based on the name of the fundraising firm, following Suhrke (2002). As expected, the special event and advertising-type solicitations were more expensive, with the median campaigns costing $0.70 and $0.75 of each dollar raised. In contrast, the donation-oriented campaigns cost $0.63 per dollar, still representing the bulk of proceeds raised.

Question 5: Does the size of the telemarketing campaign affect its cost-effectiveness?

Professional solicitors suggest that they can engage in telemarketing campaigns that charitable organizations would not be able to carry out on their own. Nonprofits with little or no fundraising staff could not undertake a complex fundraising effort that attempts to reach thousands of donors. In addition, many nonprofits do not possess the extensive mailing or calling lists that telemarketers have available to them. Therefore, phone-based professional solicitations may be a cost-effective fundraising option.

Figure 6.2. Analysis of campaign size

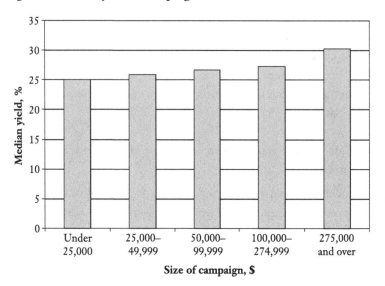

To examine the effects of campaign size, we divided the sample into five equally sized groups based on gross proceeds. Although Figure 6.2 reveals that the yields were somewhat related to the size of the fundraising campaigns, we found that the median yield to nonprofits varied little between the size categories. The biggest difference in yields was between the smallest campaigns (under $25,000), which generated a median yield of 25 percent, and the largest campaigns ($275,000 and higher), which produced a median yield of 30 percent. However, professional fundraisers were still retaining most of the funds raised for most large campaigns.

Question 6: What is the relation between yield and charity's experience in telemarketing?

Table 6.2 shows the outcomes of fundraising drives for charities with varying experience with telemarketing campaigns. A surprisingly high number of charities (405, or 9 percent of the sample) reported only one outsourced phone solicitation in New York State in the eight-year sample period. In addition, 60 percent of the campaigns raised funds for charities that averaged less than one campaign a year.

Table 6.2. Charity experience analysis

Number of Campaigns per Charity	Total Number of Campaigns	Percentage of All Campaigns	Number of Charities	Average Gross Amount Raised, $	Median Yield, %
1	405	8.5	405	91,287	20.0
2–3	768	16.1	322	147,585	25.0[a]
4–5	885	18.5	199	178,073	27.9[a]
6–7	819	17.1	126	179,292	25.0[a]
8–9	858	18.0	104	246,036	30.0[a]
10–14	430	9.0	39	647,411	30.0
15–19	278	5.8	17	584,884	31.7
20 and over	335	7.0	13	801,014	20.0[a]
Total	4,778	100.0	1,225	287,814	26.6

[a]The yield in this category of charity experience differs considerably from the yield on campaigns conducted for nonprofits with the next lower level of campaign experience.

In fact, only 173 of the 1,225 charities averaged one or more phone solicitations per year.

Professional solicitors assert that even when telemarketing campaigns are expensive, charities still benefit from the exposure they gain during the campaign. They argue that this exposure results in an increased awareness of the nonprofit organization and its mission and a refinement of the calling lists that will translate into more profitable campaigns in the future. Suhrke (2002) echoes this claim. However, it could also be argued that nonprofits will pursue telemarketing until the yields become too low.

The yield for nonprofits that conducted only one campaign was 20 percent, which is considerably lower than the 25 percent generated for groups that conducted two or three campaigns during the sample period. For charities that engaged in eight to nineteen campaigns, the yield was higher at about 30 percent. However, the yield fell to 20 percent for nonprofits that used twenty or more campaigns in the eight-year period.

The overall pattern in the reported yields is consistent with both stories. Nonprofits that engaged in an initial campaign that produced only 20 percent may have decided to forego additional solicitations, whereas the more successful ones continued until the yields began to fall. Alternatively, the pattern could be explained by a low initial interest by potential donors; these were offset over time by solicitations that were more profitable because of increased awareness or better-targeted phone lists.

Question 7: Do professional solicitors become more cost-effective as they gain fundraising experience?

One reason to hire a professional solicitor is to benefit from the fundraiser's existing lists of potential donors and expertise in fundraising methods. Therefore, professional fundraisers would be expected to become more efficient with each subsequent campaign undertaken on behalf of nonprofit organizations. Alternatively, less experienced telemarketers may be forced to offer attractive financial arrangements to attract clients.

Table 6.3 presents the cost-effectiveness of telemarketing campaigns based on the experience of the solicitor. Almost two-thirds of professional solicitors engaged in fewer than twenty campaigns during the eight-year period. Only 10 of 191 solicitors undertook an average of ten or more campaigns in New York State per year.

The campaigns were divided into six approximately equally sized groups. The less experienced telemarketers generated higher yields for their clients than the more experienced solicitors. The 121 fundraisers that conducted fewer than twenty campaigns produced virtually the same yield as the moderately experienced (with twenty

Table 6.3. Telemarketer experience analysis

Number of Campaigns per Telemarketer	Total Number of Campaigns	Number of Telemarketers	Number of Charities	Median Yield, %
1–19	781	121	343	28.8
20–39	911	32	325	30.0
40–59	878	18	315	30.0
60–84	722	10	237	25.0[a]
85–129	631	6	202	25.0
130 and over	855	4	295	24.6
Total	4,778	191	1,225	26.6

[a]The yield in this category of telemarketer experience is substantially lower than the yield on campaigns conducted by telemarketers with the next lower level of campaign experience.

to fifty-nine campaigns). However, the yield for both groups was higher than that generated by the fundraisers with sixty or more campaigns.

The reasons for this result are not clear. It could be that the less experienced are more specialized or that the more experienced are able to charge higher fees because of their reputation.

Question 8: Has the pressure from the New York State Attorney General improved the yields over time?

As indicated earlier, Attorney General Spitzer publishes a public report, "Pennies for Charities," that details the results of that year's phone solicitations. In addition, he pursued increased monitoring of the telemarketing filings in the mid- to late 1990s and recommended four reforms in 2001. As a result, increased yields might be expected to be seen over time.

As shown in Table 6.4, the median yield increased steadily from 1995 through 1999, from 25 to 30 percent. However, the yield then declined to 27 percent in 2000 and 28 percent in 2001. Year to year, there were not large changes in the yield; however, the yields for 1999 to 2001 were collectively higher than the yields for 1994 to 1998.

Given the relatively modest change in yield over time and its reversion in recent years, the evidence does not demonstrate that increased monitoring and proposed reforms have altered

Table 6.4. Telemarketing campaigns by year

Year	Number of Campaigns	Number of Charities	Number of Telemarketers	Average Gross Amount Raised, $	Average Amount Paid to Charity, $	Median Yield, %
1994	584	500	92	272,682	91,176	25.0
1995	631	522	105	256,595	96,606	25.1
1996	585	500	104	271,697	99,175	25.0
1997	630	504	103	230,905	57,623	26.0
1998	592	467	101	304,539	89,778	27.9
1999	579	475	105	335,168	96,068	29.9
2000	594	468	107	320,710	101,157	26.8
2001	583	470	109	316,900	101,217	28.2
Total	4,778	1,225	191	287,814	91,334	26.6

substantially the compensation arrangements between solicitors and charities. However, we cannot determine whether the pressure from the New York State Attorney General has improved telemarketing campaign performance relative to other states.

Discussion and conclusion

Professional solicitors offer a number of reasons to explain the high cost of their fundraising campaigns. Monitoring agencies and state attorneys general argue that donors are uninformed about the high costs of these campaigns and would be less willing to make contributions if they knew the extent to which their donations were used to compensate for-profit firms. This study explored the arguments of both sides. Using information reported to the New York State Attorney General and subsequently provided to the public annually, we discovered that the portion of charitable donations remitted to nonprofits by professional solicitors is typically less than one-third of the total funds raised. This is true for nonprofits serving a variety of causes, regardless of the size of the charitable campaign or the telemarketing experience of the solicitor and the charity. Campaigns are modestly cheaper for charities that regularly use telemarketing services than for those that use them rarely. The telemarketing experience of the professional fundraiser has relatively little bearing on the cost-effectiveness of the campaign. In fact, solicitors with less experience in New York State produced modestly better yields than their more experienced counterparts. Essentially, our study found that the environmental and organizational factors that fundraisers claim are used to price contracts have little effect on the ultimate yield earned by a charity. Although a charity's purported purpose plays a role in the success of the campaign, our findings suggest that telemarketing arrangements are (explicitly or implicitly) structured with a heavy reliance on a (high) fixed commission rate.

Our results are perplexing. If nonprofits earn so little from telemarketing campaigns, why do they undertake them? Smaller organizations may not have the staff or volunteer base to organize a special event internally. Some nonprofits do not have the financial resources to undertake a direct-mail campaign or hire a grant writer. Hence, a primarily contingency-based telemarketing campaign may be attractive. Given the recent availability of Internal Revenue Service Forms 990, it may be beneficial to determine if either explanation is empirically supported.

Similarly, if donors are so concerned about how nonprofits spend their funds, why are they willing to contribute to nonprofits through telemarketing campaigns? One explanation is that the donors who contribute through telemarketing campaigns are unaware of the high cost either because they have not seen the statistics published by New York State or other groups or because they have been misled by inaccurate nonprofit financial reports. Alternatively, the donors might be willing to give to particular causes despite the relatively high cost. If this explanation is true, it would be interesting to know if there is a more cost-effective method of identifying and retaining these donors. Finally, donors could voice their concern about nonprofits' spending practices in a survey, yet give funds when solicited because of the effectiveness of the telemarketers' solicitation. Further research could shed light on this unexplained behavior.

References

AAFRC Trust for Philanthropy. *Giving USA 2003: The Annual Report on Philanthropy for the Year 2002*. Indianapolis, IN: American Association of Fundraising Counsel, 2003.

Association of Fundraising Professionals. "Association of Fundraising Professionals Submits Amicus Brief in Ryan Case." Jan. 23, 2003, press release. 2003a. [http://www.afpnet.org/public_policy/current_issues]. Jul. 2003.

Association of Fundraising Professionals. "Final New York Fundraising Rules More Positive for Charities." Apr. 21, 2003, press release. 2003b. [http://www.afpnet.org/public_policy/current_issues]. Jul. 2003.

Bradley, B., Jansen, P., and Silverman, L. "The Nonprofit Sector's $100 Billion Opportunity." *Harvard Business Review*, 2003, *81*(5), 94–103.

Glaser, J. S. *The United Way Scandal: An Insider's Account of What Went Wrong and Why*. New York: Wiley, 1994.

Greenhouse, L. "Justices Seem to Lean to Charity Telemarketer." *New York Times*, Mar. 4, 2003, p. A18.

Greenlee, J. S., and Brown, K. L. "The Impact of Accounting Information on Contributions to Charitable Organizations." *Research in Accounting Regulation*, 1999, *13*, 111–125.

Greenlee, J. S., and Gordon, T. P. "The Impact of Professional Solicitors on Fund-Raising in Charitable Organizations." *Nonprofit and Voluntary Sector Quarterly*, 1998, *27*(3), 277–299.

Hager, M., Rooney, P., and Pollak, T. "How Fundraising Is Carried Out in US Nonprofit Organizations." *International Journal of Nonprofit and Voluntary Sector Marketing*, 2002, *7*(4), 311–324.

Lane, C. "High Court: States Can Sue Charities for Fraud." *Washington Post*, May 6, 2003, p. A4.

Princeton Survey Research Associates. *BBB Wise Giving Alliance Donor Expectations Survey: Final Report*. Princeton, N.J.: Princeton Survey Research Associates, 2001.

Strom, S. "With a Lawsuit Pending, Charities Are Divided Over Disclosure to Donors." *New York Times*, Feb. 2, 2003, p. A27.

Suhrke, H. C. "Behind the Official Figures." *Philanthropy Monthly*, 2002, *34*(5&6), 6–16.

Tinkelman, D. "Factors Affecting the Relation Between Donations to Not-for-Profit Organizations and an Efficiency Ratio." *Research in Government and Nonprofit Accounting*, 1999, *10*, 135–161.

Weisbrod, B. A., and Dominguez, N. D. "Demand for Collective Goods in Private Nonprofit Markets: Can Fundraising Expenditures Help Overcome Free-Rider Behavior?" *Journal of Public Economics*, 1986, *30*, 83–96.

ELIZABETH K. KEATING *is assistant professor of public policy at the Kennedy School of Government at Harvard University.*

LINDA M. PARSONS *is assistant professor of accounting at the School of Management at George Mason University in Fairfax, Virginia.*

ANDREA ALSTON ROBERTS *is assistant professor of accounting at the Carroll School of Management at Boston College.*

Index

Back Issue/Subscription Order Form

Copy or detach and send to:
Jossey-Bass, A Wiley Company, 989 Market Street, San Francisco CA 94103-1741

Call or fax toll-free: Phone 888-378-2537; Fax 888-481-2665

Back Issues: Please send me the following issues at $29 each
(Important: please include series initials and issue number, such as PF22)

_____

_____

$ _____   Total for single issues

$ _____   SHIPPING CHARGES: SURFACE   Domestic Canadian
                                         First Item $5.00 $6.00
                                         Each Add'l Item $3.00 $1.50
                        Please call for next day, second day, or international shipping rates.

Subscriptions   Please ❏ start ❏ renew my subscription to _New Directions for Philanthropic Fundraising_ at the following rate:

U.S.	❏ Individual $109	❏ Institutional $215
Canada	❏ Individual $109	❏ Institutional $255
All Others	❏ Individual $133	❏ Institutional $289
Online Subscription		❏ Institutional $215

**For more information about online subscriptions visit
www.interscience.wiley.com**

$ _____   Total single issues and subscriptions (Add appropriate sales tax for your state for single issue orders. No sales tax for U.S. subscriptions. Canadian residents, add GST for subscriptions and single issues.)

❏ Payment enclosed (U.S. check or money order only)
❏ VISA ❏ MC ❏ AmEx # _____ Exp. Date _____
                  Your credit card payment will be charged to John Wiley & Sons.

Signature _____ Day Phone _____
❏ Bill Me (U.S. institutional orders only. Purchase order required.)

Purchase order # _____
                  Federal Tax ID13559302   **GST 89102 8052**

Name _____

Address _____

_____

Phone _____ E-mail _____

Previous Issues Available